TREASURES *from* HOLY SCRIPTURE

T. B. MASTON

BROADMAN PRESS
Nashville, Tennessee

© Copyright 1987 ● Broadman Press
All Rights Reserved
4250-43
ISBN: 0-8054-5043-2
Dewey Decimal Classification: 242
Subject Heading: MEDITATIONS
Library of Congress Catalog Number: 86-31671
Printed in the United States of America

Library of Congress Cataloging-in-Publication Data

Maston, T. B. (Thomas Buford), 1897-
   Treasures from Holy Scripture.

   1. Bible—Criticism, interpretation, etc.
2. Bible—Meditations. I. Title.
BS511.2.M35 1987   242'.5   86-31671
ISBN 0-8054-5043-2

Contents

Old Testament

New Testament

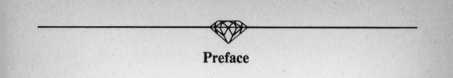

Preface

This book has been written primarily for devotional reading and study. It is hoped that many Christian youth and adults will find it helpful for their daily "quiet time" or personal devotions. Some families may find the treasures appropriate for their periods of family worship. Pastors and other speakers may discover ideas for brief devotional messages or even for an occasional sermon.

Each devotional, with only three or four exceptions, is based on a single verse of Scripture. They are representative of most of the books of the Bible and are arranged in the order of their occurrences in the Scriptures. Each has been restricted to less than one page. There is a total of 150, fifty-five from the Old Testament and ninety-five from the New Testament.

The contents lists treasure titles and Scriptures on which they are based. This should save considerable time for some readers who may be looking for material on a particular verse or subject.

A devotional approach to the Scriptures may major on messages of comfort or of challenge. While there is some attention in this book to the former, the predominant emphasis will be on the latter. Over and over again, there will be a challenge for all of us as Christians to live a more consistent life for the Lord.

I hope you will let these *Treasures from Holy Scripture* challenge you as the writing of them has challenged me.

T. B. Maston

"In the Beginning God"
(Gen. 1:1)

In the beginning God created the heavens and the earth (Gen. 1:1).

The first four words of the Bible set the tone for the biblical perspective in general. In similar words, John opens his Gospel: "In the beginning was the Word, and the Word was with God, and the Word was God" (John 1:1). God, not humanity, was and is the beginning of His creative and re-creative, redemptive work.

God should be the point of reference for every area of the life of the individual child of God and also for the church and the nation.

What place do we give to God in our family relations, our church, our daily work, our recreation, and life in general? Is He at the beginning or the end? first or last? at the center of the circumference?

Do we start with Him at the beginning of the day? Is He the One from whom we seek counsel about daily decisions?

The place we give to God in our lives will make a tremendous difference in the quality of life we live for Him and for our fellow human beings. There is no better place to begin this series than with the four words: "In the beginning God"!

Evening and Morning
(Gen. 1:5)

The evening and the morning were the first day (Gen. 1:5, KJV).

Each of the creative days closes with the same statement: "And the evening and the morning were . . ." We would say "the morning and the evening." For the Jews the day began with sunset; for us it begins with sunrise.

Could it be that "evening and morning" suggests or at least implies God's perspective regarding time? It seems that for Him morning follows evening, sunshine comes after darkness and drives the shadows away.

Whether or not we can base this perspective on the Creation account, it is true of the experience of many Christians. Many of us are grateful that when the evenings of darkness come, they are followed by the mornings of additional light and insight. Sometimes we have discovered that the darker the night, the brighter the light of the morning.

Also, how glorious it is to remember that morning follows the evening as life slips away from a loved one or a friend. For many of them the evening of suffering has been followed by the brightness of God's morning.

Death is sometimes compared to a door. If so, it is a swinging door: not only a door *out* of something but also *into* life in its fullness with our Lord. Morning comes as surely as the evening.

"In the Image of God"
(Gen. 1:26-27)

Then God said, "Let us make man in our image, . . ." So God created man in his own image, in the image of God he created him; male and female he created them (Gen. 1:26-27).

The most significant thing about humans is that they were created in the image of God. What does this mean?

One thing it clearly means is that since God is a Person, a human being is also a person. Persons can think, feel, and will. They have the capacity for self-knowledge and self-determination.

A most important characteristic of a person is the fact that his very nature demands communication with other persons. In other words, in reality there is no person without other persons. The highest expression of the need for communication is human fellowship with God.

It is particularly important for human relations that all people are created in the image of God. In the beginning, it says: "Male and female created he them." Men and women are equally created in the image of God. The same can be said for those of different racial or cultural groups.

Those who have been created in the image of God should always be respected as ends of infinite value and never as mere means. They should never be manipulated or used to attain selfish ends.

"Where Are You?"
(Gen. 3:9)

The Lord God called to the man, and said to him, "Where are you?" (Gen. 3:9).

An examination of questions asked and/or recorded in the Bible would make an interesting and profitable study. This would be true of human questions to God, as well as God's questions to humans. "Where are you?" is the first recorded question that God asked man.

This is a question that God, through the centuries, has continued to ask men and women. He is on a constant search. If we had the ears to hear, we would hear Him persistently asking, "Where are you?"

Where are we in relation to Him—to His will and purpose for us?

Where are we in our devotion to Him and His cause? Do we love Him supremely? Do we seek first His kingdom?

Where are we in relation to His church and our church? Are we faithful to its services and programs?

Where are we in relation to the members of our family? to neighbors? to those with whom we work? to men and women of other colors, classes, and cultures?

Where are we in personal spiritual growth and maturity? Are we letting the resurrected Christ live in us and express Himself more fully through us from day to day?

Disobedience and Fear
(Gen. 3:10)

And he said, "I heard the sound of thee [as you were walking, NEB] in the garden, and I was afraid, because I was naked; and I hid myself" (Gen. 3:10).

Why was Adam afraid? Why did he hide from God when God called, "Where are you"? Adam was afraid because he had disobeyed God.

Will you not agree that just as God continues to search for all, so the reaction of Adam continues to be the reaction of sinful people? This is even true of those of us who are Christians; we, in reality, are

13

saved sinners. We seek to hide from His presence when we have been disobedient to Him, to His way and will for our lives.

Christians seek in various ways to hide from God. Some drop out of church; others even slip back into the sins they participated in before they came to know the Lord.

Is it not the experience of all of us who know Him as our Heavenly Father that we cannot escape His searching? We may seek to hide from Him, but we cannot. He will sooner or later find us and face us with our sins. He will not force us to be obedient to Him, but we can be sure that we will be afraid of His presence until we respond to His searching.

Just as disobedient children are fearful of the presence of their parents, so the disobedient child of God is afraid of Him and seeks to hide from Him.

Sin Separates
(Gen. 3:23)

Therefore the Lord God sent [drove, NEB] him forth from the garden of Eden (Gen. 3:23).

There is an abiding lesson in this experience of Adam and Eve in the Garden of Eden: sin separates one from God.

We know, of course, that sin separates the unsaved from God. They cannot come into the presence of God and feel the touch of His redeeming love until they repent of their sins.

It is equally as true, however, that sin in the life of the Christian separates one from God. To the degree that we have unforgiven sin in our lives, to that degree we will be separated from our Heavenly Father.

The preceding means, among other things, that if we are not conscious of His presence, we should examine and see if sin has crept into our lives. As has been frequently and truly said, sin separates us from God, or God separates us from sin.

But, also, sin not only separates us from God but also separates us from our fellow human beings. Sin will separate us in every relationship of life—in the home, in the church, in the neighborhood, in the school, in the business world—everywhere.

"My Brother's Keeper"
(Gen. 4:9)

Then the Lord said to Cain, "Where is Abel your brother?" He said, "I do not know; am I my brother's keeper?" (Gen. 4:9).

This one verse contains two significant and continuing relevant questions. The first is a question that God not only asked then but has continued to ask it through the centuries. He would ask you and me: Where is your brother?—your blood brother, your Christian brother, your brother of various races and colors.

In turn Cain asked God a question that people through the centuries have continued to ask: "Am I my brother's keeper?"

God did not answer Cain directly. He seldom answers our questions directly. His reply to Cain, however, was plainly and pointedly "Yes." He would say to you and me, particularly to those of us in His spiritual family, "You are your brother's keeper." We are responsible to God for our relations to our brothers and sisters, for how we treat them, what we do for and to them.

And we should remember that our Heavenly Father is no respecter of persons. He expects us to manifest His spirit and attitude in all of our relations, not only with fellow Christians but with men and women in general. After all, we are equally created in the image of God, and Christ died for all.

Purpose of God's Blessings
(Gen. 12:2)

I will bless you, . . . so that you will be a blessing (Gen. 12:2).

These words were addressed to Abram (Abraham). God promised, "I will make of you a great nation." In turn, Abraham and his dependents would be a great blessing. This was a simple statement of fact: God would bless Abraham, and the latter in turn *would be* a blessing.

The same can and should be true of every child of God. If we will open our lives to Him, He will bless us, and to the degree that He blesses us, we will be a blessing to those whose lives we touch.

There is a closely related truth that can be implied from this Scripture. God's children of the present, as of the past, are responsible to Him for the blessings they receive from Him. In other words, His blessings are a part of our stewardship responsibility.

In a sense, God's blessings to us are preparatory. They should create in us a desire to be a blessing to those we touch in our homes, our churches, on the street, or anywhere we contact people.

What is true for individuals should also be true of a church or a nation. They, like we, are responsible to God for any blessings they have received from Him.

Holy Ground
(Ex. 3:5)

Then he said, "Do not come near; put off your shoes [sandals] from your feet, for the place on which you are standing is holy ground" (Ex. 3:5).

These words were spoken by God to Moses at the burning bush. What made it holy ground? It was the presence of the Lord. Any place where we meet God is holy.

There God revealed to Moses (1) who He was: "the God of your father, the God of Abraham, . . . Isaac, . . . Jacob" (v. 6); (2) His concern for His people: "I have seen the affliction of my people" (v. 7); (3) what He wanted Moses to do: "I will send you . . . that you may bring forth my people" (v. 10).

Do you and I have some "holy places" in our lives? Have there been times when we were unusually conscious of the presence of God, when we understood His concern for people and heard His call to respond to His will for our lives?

Such experiences may have come to us when we were alone in our homes or in God's vast outdoors. Or we may have been in a worship service in our church or in a period of family worship. Wherever we were, the place was made holy by the unusual sense of God's presence.

Do you have memories of such holy places in your life? More importantly, are you and I conscious of His presence as we go about our tasks today?

A God Who Hears
(Ex. 3:7-8)

Then the Lord said, "I have seen the affliction of my people who are in Egypt, and have heard their cry because of their taskmasters; I know their sufferings, and I have come down to deliver them out of the hand of the Egyptians, and to bring them up out of that land to a good and broad land, a land flowing with milk and honey, to the place of the Canaanites, the Hittites, the Amorites, the Perizzites, the Hivites, and the Jebusites" (Ex. 3:7-8).

Notice the verbs in these verses: "I have seen . . . have heard . . . know . . . have come down . . . to bring them up." That is typical of our Heavenly Father. He has through the centuries heard the cry of His children. He knows their burdens and problems, but how grateful we ought to be that He does not only see and hear and know, but He "comes down" to encourage and to relieve.

Sometimes the relief He gives to His contemporary children is an inner victory over the conditions that would defeat them.

What about those of us who have had the relief or the victory that comes from a touch of His Spirit on our spirits? Are we as thankful as we should be? How do we express our gratitude?

Have we heard, or do we hear the cry of suffering humanity in our community and in our world?

What about our churches? Do they hear? Do they seek to be channels of our Heavenly Father's compassion and concern?

Peace by a Presence
(Ex. 33:14)

And he said, "My presence will go with you, and I will give you rest" (Ex. 33:14).

Many of us need the same assurance that God gave to Moses. We need to sense His presence to set our minds at rest (NEB).

Some things tend to rob us of the quiet and peace we should have. We may live at too hurried a pace. We may be disturbingly conscious about falling short of what we know we ought to be—and even what others may think we are.

There may be tensions and problems in our homes and where we work. Conditions in our churches and in the world may at times, and should, deeply concern us.

There are some things we can do ourselves to have the inner peace we desire and need. The most significant source, however, for the peace that passes understanding is simply to rest or "let go" in the Lord. The sense of His presence can be a source of peace not dependent on external conditions.

Years ago I read an illustration that has meant much to me. An elderly lady had hurried to catch a commuter train to take her garden produce to the market. The train was crowded. She had to stand, holding her heavy basket on her arm. A kindly young man touched her elbow and suggested, "Ma'am, put your basket down. The train will carry it and you."

May we cultivate the capacity to let the Lord carry us and our burdens.

"You Shall Be Holy"
(Lev. 19:2)

You shall be holy; for I the Lord your God am holy (Lev. 19:2).

Many terms are used in the Scriptures to describe the nature and character of God. None is more central or more inclusive than His holiness.

It is consistently revealed in the Scriptures that God wants His people to be like Him. What is written concerning holiness could be said concerning every other quality that is used to describe God: His righteousness, justice, love, mercy, and faithfulness.

To be holy means basically to be separated or to be set apart. When the term *holy* is applied to people, the idea has both negative and positive aspects. A verse from Leviticus sets out clearly these two aspects of holiness: "You shall be holy to me; for I the Lord am holy, and have separated you from the peoples, that you should be mine" (Lev. 20:26). "Separated you from the peoples" is the negative aspect. "Holy to me" and "that you should be mine" express the positive aspect of holiness.

Peter admonished those to whom he wrote, "As he who called you is holy, be holy yourselves in all your conduct" (1 Pet. 1:15; see 2:9) and then quoted Leviticus 19:2. How thoroughly are we separated from the world and the things of the world? How much are we separated unto God and His purposes in our lives and in our world?

Teach Children Diligently
(Deut. 6:6-7)

These words which I command you this day shall be upon your heart; and you shall teach them diligently to your children (Deut. 6:6-7).

What were the "words" the Israelites were commanded to teach their children? The immediate reference was to the preceding words: "You shall love the Lord your God with all your heart, and with all your soul, and with all your might" (Deut. 6:5). This statement was quoted by Jesus when He was asked for the great commandment in the law. It is possible that "these words which I command you" refers to the Commandments and statutes of God in general (see vv. 1-2).

"Diligently" is spelled out to some degree. They were to talk of the Commandments of God as they sat in their houses, as they walked in the way, when they lay down, and when they arose. They were to bind them for signs upon their hands and as frontlets between their eyes. They were to be written upon the posts of the house and on the gates.

A significant part of this statement is frequently overlooked. It says: "These words . . . shall be upon your heart." This precedes "You shall teach them diligently to your children." Parents cannot effectively teach their children to love God supremely or to keep His Command-

ments in general unless they seek to practice in their own lives what
they would teach their children.

Demonstration is the most effective method of teaching.

God's Requirements
(Deut. 10:12-13)

Now, Israel, what does the Lord your God require of you, but to fear
the Lord your God, to walk in all his ways, to love him, to serve the
Lord your God with all your heart and with all your soul, and to keep
the commandments and statutes of the Lord, which I command you
this day for your good? (Deut. 10:12-13).

There are a number of places in the Scriptures where the requirements of God are presented or summarized. In places these are God's
expectations of the individual child of God. More frequently, however, the reference is to the nation. Even where the reference is to the
nation, the requirements of God can properly be applied to the individual child of God.

Notice in these verses how clearly God's requirements are delin-
eated. Let us use the present tense and apply these verses to us and
to our nation. God expects us to "fear" or reverence Him, to walk in
or be conformed (NEB) to His way, to love Him—an emphasis found
in Deuteronomy more than in any other Old Testament book—to
serve Him with all our hearts and souls, our total personalities, and
to keep His Commandments.

The New English Bible makes the last one a separate sentence:
"This [fear God, walk in His way, love Him, serve Him] you will do
by keeping the commandments of the Lord."

Notice one another important idea: the Commandments of God are
for our good and for the good of our nation. Jesus said: "The sabbath
was made for man, not man for the sabbath" (Mark 2:27). Every
commandment or expectation of God is for our good. No wonder
John said, "His commandments are not burdensome" (John 5:3).

Divorce: Real and Ideal
(Deut. 24:1; Mal. 2:16)

> When a man takes a wife . . . if then she finds no favor in his eyes
> . . . he writes her a bill of divorce, . . . and sends her out of his house
> (Deut. 24:1).

> For the Lord, the God of Israel, saith that He hateth putting away
> (Mal. 2:16, KJV).

These verses reveal the attitude toward divorce in the Old Testament. The law sought to regulate divorce which was more or less prevelant. In contrast, Malachi said that God hated "putting away" (KJV) or divorce.

There is additional evidence in the Old Testament which reveals that God disapproved of divorce. For example, the priest and high priest were not to marry one who had been put away (Lev. 21:7,14). Why? "For [the priest] is holy unto his God." This implied that there was something unholy about one who had been divorced.

If God hated divorce, why was there provision for divorce in the law? Jesus plainly taught it was because of the hardness of heart of the people (Matt. 19:8). When God through Moses provided some regulation of divorce, He sought to meet the needs of the people where they were. At the same time, the ideal unquestionably was one man and one woman as husband and wife for life.

Such balancing of the real and the ideal is relevant for us today. If we minister effectively to people, we must uncompromisingly preach and teach the ideal, but as we counsel and work with individuals we must seek as best we can to meet their immediate needs. We must start where they are.

Caleb's Request
(Josh. 14:12)

> So now give me this hill country of which the Lord spoke on that day;
> for you heard on that day how the Anakim were there, with great
> fortified cities (Josh. 14:12).

What is the background for Caleb's "So now" or "Now therefore" (KJV)? Joshua was dividing the land that God had given the children of Israel. Caleb mentioned to Joshua that Moses had promised him the land "on which your foot has trodden" (v. 9). That promise was when Caleb and Joshua were the only spies who encouraged the people to enter in and possess that land.

Caleb also mentioned the fact that he was "fourscore and five years old" (KJV). It would have seemed logical for him to have asked Joshua to give him the fertile valleys.

Caleb's request, however, was for "hill country" or "this mountain" (KJV). And he knew that the "Anakim [giants] were there." His conclusion was: "It may be that the Lord will be with me, and I shall drive them out as the Lord said."

Two or three facts are evident in Caleb's life that apply to all of us. There was no evidence that he was jealous of Joshua. Also, Caleb's life at eighty-five was simply an extension of his life at forty; he was as courageous at eight-five as he was at forty. Also, Caleb was not ready to be put on the shelf. There was no retirement for him.

Too many older people in our churches and in society in general are put on the shelf prematurely.

A Challenge
(Josh. 24:15)

Choose this day whom you will serve, . . . but as for me and my house, we will serve the Lord (Josh. 24:15).

These words were spoken by Joshua. He had led in the conquest of the Promised Land. He was nearing the end of his life. He called a meeting of the leaders of Israel, reviewing briefly the history of God's dealings with the children of Israel.

From that kind of background Joshua challenged them to choose whom they would serve. He then pointedly asserted, "But as for me and my house, we will serve the Lord." That would be true of him and his family regardless of what others might do.

The challenge was greater because these were the words of an old and respected leader. Many homes and churches need men who will courageously say, "As for me and my house . . ."

These words and this challenge also came from the leader of the children of Israel. Many communities, states, and nations need leaders who will have the courage to say, "As for me and my house . . ."

Leaders who will stand for God and right will usually discover that people will respond to their challenge and courage. The reply of the children of Israel was: "The Lord our God we will serve, and his voice we will obey" (v. 24; see vv. 16,18,21). A courageous soul will rarely have to stand alone.

And Gideon
(Judg. 7:20)

A sword for the Lord and for Gideon! (Judg. 7:20, NASB).

These words provided the climax of a unique Old Testament stories. Gideon, following God's instructions, had reduced the number of the children of Israel going up against the Midianites. Gideon had started with several thousand but he had reduced the number until he had only three-hundred men.

A careful strategy was planned. They divided into three companies of one-hundred men each. They were placed on different sides of the camp of the Midianites. At a signal they all blew their trumpets, and holding up their torches, they cried, "A sword for the Lord and for Gideon!"

Why is "for Gideon" or "of Gideon" added? Could the Lord have won the victory without Gideon? Yes and no. He could have, but that is not the way He operated then or operates now.

God uses human instrumentality to accomplish His work in the world. He wants to reach people around us, but He will not do it except through us.

On the other hand, let us never forget that we cannot do His work in the world without His help.

If we recognize that God works with and through us, it will save us from two self-defeating attitudes. It will rescue us from a sense of inferiority which adversely affects many of God's children. It will also deliver us from a sense of self-sufficiency and self-importance.

We are, or are supposed to be, instruments of God in His work in the world.

Obedience
(1 Sam. 15:22)

Behold, to obey is better than sacrifice, and to hearken than the fat of rams (1 Sam. 15:22).

These words were spoken by Samuel to Saul. The king and the people had failed to be obedient to the Lord. Instead of destroying everything as commanded, they had saved some of the sheep and oxen, so Saul claimed, "To sacrifice unto the Lord your God in Gilgal" (v. 21). Notice "your God"—He was definitely the God of Samuel.

Then Samuel reaffirmed the continuing emphasis of God's prophets that obedience is better than sacrifice. In other words, the kind of worship acceptable unto God involves obedience.

This basic message of the prophets is fully as applicable today as in Samuel's day. Regardless of how faithful we are in following the prescribed forms of worship, our worship will not be acceptable to the righteous and Holy God unless it is accompanied with and motivated by obedience.

And we should never forget that the kind of obedience God expects of His children involves something of His spirit and attitude toward people. This involves relations in the home, with fellow church members, neighbors, friends, and even enemies.

How do we measure up?

A Temple in the Heart
(1 Kings 8:17-18)

Now it was in the heart of David . . . to build a house [temple, NIV] for the name of the Lord, the God of Israel. But the Lord said to David . . . "Whereas it was in your heart to build a house for my name, you did well that it was in your heart" (1 Kings 8:17-18).

The main thrust of these verses is the fact that God approved

David's desire to build the Temple. David, however, was not permitted to build the Temple because he was a warrior and had shed much blood (1 Chron. 28:3). This implies that war and the shedding of blood were not and are not in harmony with God's perfect or intentional will. But God approved the idea or desire that David had to build His Temple.

Many saints of God through the centuries have had it in their hearts to accomplish great things for God. They may have been unable, through no fault of their own, to do so. Their dreams may have been in harmony with God's purpose and will, but for various reasons those dreams never became realities. We believe that God would say to such saints of His, "Whereas it was in your heart . . . you did well."

We can be assured that if the dream we have in our hearts is in harmony with the purpose of God He will say to us as He did to David, "Whereas . . ."

It is better to dream dreams for God, dreams that may never become realities, than not to dream at all.

"A Still Small Voice"
(1 Kings 19:12)

And after the earthquake a fire, but the Lord was not in the fire; and after the fire a still small voice (1 Kings 19:12).

After his and the Lord's victory over the prophets of Baal, Elijah had run from the anger of Jezebel, the queen. He finally ended up in a cave "a long, long ways from home."

There in the cave the prophet heard the question of the Lord, "What are you doing here, Elijah?"—a question that He may be asking you and me. After Elijah had explained why he was there, the Lord commanded, "Go forth, and stand upon the mount before the Lord" (v. 11).

There God revealed Himself to Elijah in a rather unexpected way. A great and strong wind passed by but "the Lord was not in the wind." After the wind there was an earthquake, and after the earthquake a fire, but the Lord did not speak to Elijah from the earthquake or the fire.

Then God spoke to Elijah in "a still small voice" (v. 12), "a sound of a gentle blowing" (NASB), "a low murmuring sound" (NEB), or "a gentle whisper" (NIV). This is how the Lord frequently continues to speak to His children.

After listening to Elijah's review of what had happened to him, the Lord instructed, "Go, return" and then gave him instructions about what he was to do as he returned.

There is always something to do about any new vision or fresh insight from the Lord.

The Prophet Speaks
(1 Kings 22:14)

What the Lord says to me, that I will speak (1 Kings 22:14).

These words were spoken by Micaiah, a little-known prophet of God. Jehoshaphat, king of Judah, and Ahab, king of Israel, were considering an attempt to take Ramoth-gilead from Syria. Four-hundred so-called prophets of Israel had said, "Go up; for the Lord will give it into the hand of the king" (v. 6).

Jehoshaphat asked if there were not another prophet of whom they might inquire. Ahab reported that there was a prophet named Micaiah. However, the king added, "But I hate him, for he never prophesies good concerning me, but evil" (v. 8).

A messenger was sent to bring Micaiah. The messenger told Micaiah about the favorable report of the four-hundred prophets. He suggested that Micaiah should also speak favorably about the proposed project. Then it was that Micaiah said, "What the Lord says to me, that I will speak," or "I can tell him only what the Lord tells me" (NIV).

In the presence of Jehoshaphat and Ahab, Micaiah predicted the failure of the venture and even the death of Ahab. The angered king ordered God's prophet to be put in prison and to be placed on a "scant fare of bread and water" (v. 27) until the king returned in peace.

The words of the prophet, possibly spoken as they led him away, were, "If you return in peace, the Lord has not spoken by me" (v. 28). What courage! What a prophet! We need more prophets in the pulpit and pew who will declare, "What the Lord says to me, that I will speak."

Three Searching Questions
(2 Kings 4:26)

Is it well with you? Is it well with your husband? Is it well with the child (the boy, NEB) (2 Kings 4:26).

The son that Elisha had promised the Shunammite woman had died. While on her way to Elisha, he saw her coming. He told his servant Gehazi to go and meet her and ask her three searching questions. I do not believe we will do any violence to this Scripture if we apply it to contemporary wives and mothers.

Is it well with you, with your attitude toward yourself? Is it well with you as wife and mother? As neighbor and friend? As citizen and church member? Is it well with you in relation to your Lord and His work in the world?

Is it well with your husband? Are his physical and emotional needs properly provided for in the home? Are you a help or a hindrance to him in his chosen vocation or profession? What about his relationship to the Lord and to the Lord's church and cause?

Is it well with the child or children? Have you and their father provided a wholesome and stimulating intellectual, emotional, and spiritual atmosphere for them? Is there a sincere effort to understand their problems? Do you genuinely and wisely love them?

These are only a relatively few questions that could be asked. Similar questions could be appropriately asked husbands and fathers.

Personal Touch
(2 Kings 4:34)

Then he [Elisha] . . . lay upon the child, . . . and as he stretched himself upon him, the flesh of the child became warm (2 Kings 4:34).

You know the rest of the story. Elisha has sent Gehazi ahead and had instructed him to place Elisha's staff on the dead child. The mother, however, would not leave without Elisha. Gehazi met them before they got there and told Elisha, "The child has not awakened" (v. 31).

Elisha went into the room that had been provided for him where the dead child was lying on his bed. He lay upon the child, mouth to mouth, eye to eye, hand to hand. Then it was that the child became warm. He stretched himself again on the child, and life returned.

There is an important lesson in this incident. There is no substitute for the personal touch. Elisha's staff would not bring life back into the body of the dead child.

So it is in our day in the work of the Lord. There is no substitute for personal involvement. This is true in our search for the unsaved in our community. It is also true in any effort to be of help to the lonely and hurting. They need someone to touch them and bring them new life and hope.

Do you not agree that too frequently we and our churches try to substitute material things for the personal touch?

God's Also
(2 Chron. 1:12)

Wisdom and knowledge are granted to you. I will also give you riches, possessions, and honor, such as none of the kings had who were before you, and none after you shall have the like (2 Chron. 1:12).

Solomon's God, who is also our God, was and is generous. He gave Solomon more than he asked for. God had appeared to Solomon and had said to him, "Ask what I shall give you" (v. 7). Solomon requested that the Lord to give him wisdom and knowledge, which were his greatest need as successor of David, his father, as king.

Then God added an "also." In His response, God said that He would not only give Solomon the wisdom and knowledge he had requested but would also give him what he had not asked for: riches, possessions, and honor!

You and I are not kings. We are not rulers over people, but we worship the same God who responded so generously to Solomon. Our Heavenly Father will provide blessings far beyond anything we ask for or expect. This will definitely be true if we pray unselfishly and within His will.

God's "alsos" are not only applicable in the area of prayer. We will discover in many of our relationships with Him that there ultimately will be an "also." For example, if we give ourselves unselfishly to His way and will, we will discover sooner or later the maximum fulfillment of every basic need and desire of our lives.

Restoring Altars
(2 Chron. 33:16)

He also restored the altar of the Lord and offered upon it sacrifices of peace offerings and of thanksgiving; and he commanded Judah to serve the Lord the God of Israel (2 Chron. 33:16).

Manasseh had built altars to foreign gods and had neglected the altar of the Lord. As a captive in Babylon he humbled himself before the Lord and prayed, and the Lord brought him back to Jerusalem. One of his acts was to restore the altar of the Lord.

What about our nation: Has the altar of the Lord been neglected? Have you and I neglected the altar or the worship of the Lord?

One may regularly attend church worship services and yet worship foreign gods. This will be so if we believe that regular attendance will make us right with our God, regardless of the kind of life we live in the home, at the office, the place of business, or on the street.

Worship that does not eventually lead to service for Him and to our fellow human beings will not be acceptable to God.

Anything to which we attach supreme value becomes in a real sense our *god* and the object of our worship. What are some of those potentially false gods?—Money and material things but also position and prestige.

Whatever may be the false gods that threaten us, we should never forget that we cannot worship false gods and the true God at the same time. Also, we should recognize that we tend to become like what or whom we worship.

Effective Teaching
(Ezra 7:10)

Ezra had set his heart to study the law of the Lord, and to do it, and
to teach his statutes and ordinances in Israel (Ezra 7:10).

Ezra was one of the wise teachers of Israel. This verse reveals the
secret to his strength as a teacher. There are lessons here for all of us
but particularly for those who teach the Word of the Lord.

Notice that he "set his heart" or "devoted himself to the study"
(NIV). He had a sense of purpose or commitment. One does not
become a great or good teacher by accident. Then notice there are
three things Ezra had set his heart to do. Each is expressed by an
infinitive. They are arranged in logical order.

(1) He "set his heart *to study the law of the Lord*" (author's italics).
It takes hard work to be a good teacher—in public schools, in Sunday
School, or in any other type of teaching.

(2) Ezra "set his heart . . . *to do it*"; that is, to be obedient to what
he discovered in his study. Here is a great truth that applies to parents
as well as teachers. And after all, parents are the chief educators of
their children. We—parents and other teachers—cannot teach effectively any truth that we do not seek to apply in our own lives.

(3) Ezra set his heart *to teach the law to others.* Only after we have
studied and applied the truth to our own lives are we adequately
prepared to teach that truth to others. There will be a natural urge,
however, to share it with others.

Balancing the Divine and Human
(Neh. 4:9)

And we prayed to our God, and set a guard as a protection against
them day and night (Neh. 4:9).

Nehemiah and the children of Israel were rebuilding the walls of
Jerusalem. Their success, as is frequently true, aroused the anger of
their enemies who plotted against them.

We find in this verse the balancing of the divine and the human—
they prayed but also "set a guard." Someone has observed, "Pray like
everything depends on God; work like everything depends on you."

30

It is quite evident that God expects His children to help answer their own prayers. We are to use the resources that are available.

There is no area where this combination of the divine and human is more evident than in the area of sickness and health. It is apparent that the Lord expects us to use what is available to keep our bodies in good condition. He also expects us to use the resources open to us in times of illness: medicine, doctors, nurses, hospitals, and so forth. At the same time, we can and should pray, believing that God will make those resources more effective than if we had not prayed.

So it is in every area of our lives. For example, God reveals His will, with possibly some exceptions, only to the searching mind and the willing heart.

A People of the Book
(Neh. 8:5)

And Ezra opened the book in the sight of all the people, . . . and when he opened it all the people stood (Neh. 8:5).

Verses 1 through 8 need to be read to grasp the proper setting for this verse. The book that Ezra opened was "the book of the law of Moses" (v. 1). The people wanted to hear it. They took the initiative.

"Men and women and all who could hear with understanding" (v. 2) were present for the reading. They were willing to listen as Ezra read "from early morning until miday" (v. 3). Also, "all the people were attentive to the book of the law" (v. 3). Then it says "when he opened [the book . . . all the people stood" (v. 5)—a practice that is followed in some churches today when the Scriptures are read.

And Ezra had some helpers who "read from the book . . . clearly, made its sense plain and gave instruction in what was read" (v. 8, NEB). No individual, church, or group of people can really be a people of the Book (the Bible) unless they understand what the Book teaches.

A final test of whether or not we are a people of the Book is what happens after we hear it read and understand what it says. We can be a people who know the Book theoretically and yet reveal little of its teachings and spirit in our daily lives.

Are we *truly a people of the Book?*

Changeless in a Changing World
(Job 9:9)

Who made the Bear and Orion [constellations, NIV], the Pleiades and
the chambers of the south (Job 9:9)?

Have you ever visited a place where you lived many years ago? If
so, you were doubtlessly impressed with the many changes that had
taken place. This was particularly true if that place were in the city.
A few weeks, or even a few days, can make noticeable differences.

There are other changes in our contemporary world more telling
than the material ones. There have been in recent years rather drastic
changes in the styles of dress for both men and women. There have
also been noticeable changes in life-styles in general. Some types of
conduct formerly considered wrong are now rather generally accepted
as all right.

It may be a source of encouragement to you, as it has been to me,
to go out at night and look up at Orion, Pleiades, and other constella-
tions of the stars. The planets and stars that are up there now were
there in the days of Job and Amos (see Amos 5:8).

It is even more assuring to remember that behind the changelessness of Orion and Pleiades is the changeless God. He is the same
yesterday, today, and forever. He is the great "I Am."

An understanding of the changelessness of much of God's creation,
and particularly of His changelessness, will help to stabilize our souls.
We can have quiet and peace in the midst of the changes and uncer-
tainties of our world.

Hearing and Seeing
(Job 42:5-6)

I had heard of thee by the hearing of the ear, but now my eye sees thee;
therefore I despise myself, and repent in dust and ashes (Job 42:5-6).

A succession of tragedies had come to Job. His friends came to
console and comfort him. Each of them along with Elihu, the young-

est man, expressed the common Jewish perspective, which is still quite prevalent, that there was and is a direct connection between suffering and sin. Job, to varying degrees, defended his innocence.

Finally, God spoke to Job "out of the whirlwind" (38:1). This was the background for Job's statement, "I had heard of thee by the hearing of the ear,/but now my eye sees thee." In other words, through his suffering and God's speaking to him, his knowledge of God and God's relationship to suffering was now firsthand. It was not something that his friends or anyone else had told him. He now had a direct, personal awareness of the presence and the nature of God that could not be known simply by what others might say about God.

Also notice in the sixth verse Job's reaction to that direct awareness of the presence of God. His reaction is introduced with a "therefore," an important word in both Testaments.

Is it not true that when a person, Christian or non-Christian, feels the touch of God and hears a word from Him, the person will immediately be conscious of how unworthy he is to stand in the presence of the holy God?

Pollution and Christian Stewardship
(Ps. 24:1)

The earth is the Lord's and the fulness thereof (Ps. 24:1).

These words provide a solid basis for the stewardship of the soil. An emphasis on this aspect of stewardship was particularly relevant when we were a predominantly rural nation. It still applies directly to those who live on a farm and indirectly to all of us.

But what about the stewardship of the air and water in the contemporary world? The air, water, and the land are all a part of God's creation. It is increasingly evident that what is done in the next few years concerning the pollution of land, air, and water will determine to a considerable degree whether or not human beings will have a future on the earth.

As a phase of the fight against pollution, Christian churches should include pollution of the earth, air, and water as an integral phase of

Christian stewardship. God holds us responsible for what we do with God's gifts. Land, air, and water are among His best gifts. If these and other gifts of God are abused, judgment will come, and that judgment will not be arbitrary. It will come as the result of the way things inevitably work. The judgment or punishment is not external to the thing done. Rather, it is inherent in the act. It is a part of the operation of the laws of nature.

The Non-Fretful Heart
(Ps. 37:1)

Fret not yourself because of the wicked (Ps. 37:1).

This admonition by the psalmist is followed by a reason why we should not be fretful concerning evildoers. They may prosper, but "they will soon fade like the grass,/and wither like the green herb" (v. 2).

There are suggested in the psalm positive cures for or preventives of the fretful heart or life. These cures are expressed in the verbs that stand at the beginning of verses 3, 4, 5, and 7. Notice that they are: "Trust in the Lord," "Take delight in the Lord," "Commit your way to the Lord," "Be still before the Lord," and "wait patiently for him."

Those who trust in the Lord, delight in or "depend upon" him (NEB), commit their way or life (NEB) to the Lord, and have developed the capacity to "Rest in the Lord" (KJV) will be free from the frets and worries that disturb many people.

Really, all of these statements are closely interrelated. If we trust the Lord we will delight in Him, be willing to commit our way to Him, and can and will rest in Him or wait for Him.

How much do you and I have these qualities in our lives? If we have them they will not only give us inner peace or quiet, they will also make us more effective in our life and work for the Lord and for our fellow human beings.

How Much Do Our Hearts Weigh?
(Prov. 21:2)

Every way of a man is right in his own eyes, but the Lord weighs the heart (Prov. 21:2).

God does not necessarily accept our judgment of our conduct. "The Lord fixes a standard for the heart" (NEB).

Let us use this statement of the wise man to ask ourselves the searching question: How much do our hearts weigh? We are not talking here about "heavy hearts" in the ordinary sense. God's scales are not ours. He may weigh our hearts by our burdens and sorrows but even more by the burdens and sorrows of others that we carry.

Let us ask several questions: How many people do we carry in our hearts? Who are they? Some of them doubtlessly are relatives and friends. Are any of them people who cannot repay us for anything we give to them and do for them? Are some of them "God's special protégés": the widowed, the orphaned, and the social outcasts?

How big are our hearts? Do we include in them a love and concern for the peoples of the world? for people of all classes and colors? Do we see those people through the eyes of God who is no respecter of persons?

God weighs the heart. How much does your heart and mine weigh? He looks on the inside rather than the outside. How do you suppose we look to Him?

Impact of a Sentence
(Prov. 21:2)

A word fitly spoken is like apples of gold in a setting of silver (Prov. 25:11).

Has your life been unusually influenced by an occasional statement that someone made to you? Let me share with you only two statements that have served as a "word fitly spoken" to me.

I had been elected captain of the football team for my senior year in high school. I had been a Christian about a year. Also, I had felt called to special Christian service. The behavior of some of the fellows on the team, including their language, was terrible. The coach could or would not do anything about it. I decided that I could not take it any longer. I resigned as captain and quit the team.

Miss Gresham, my favorite teacher, sent word that she wanted to see me. In the course of our conversation she asked a question that I have never forgotten: "Do you think Jesus would quit because the going was hard?" I went back to the team that afternoon.

Miss Lucy was a tremendous friend of young people. She came to hear me attempt to preach my first sermon at my home church (I am not an ordained minister). After an awkward and unsuccessful service, and after everyone had left except my family, Miss Lucy said, "Tom, the greatest sermon you will ever preach will be the life you live." I have never gotten away from the impact of that statement. The same could be said not only of every preacher but of everyone of us who claims to be a child of God. The greatest message we will ever deliver will be the lives we live.

"A Child Left to Himself"
(Prov. 29:15)

The rod and reproof give wisdom, but a child left to himself [who gets his own way, NASB] brings shame to [disgraces, NIV] his mother (Prov. 29:15).

"Left to himself" portrays a horse that is turned loose in the pasture to roam where it will. *The New English Bible* translates the last portion of the verse as follows: "A boy who runs wild brings shame on his mother."

Do you know not only boys but also girls that are left to themselves to run wild? If you have had an occasion to drive through a town or into the city late at night you may have seen teenage youngsters who have been turned loose to roam at will. Some may be quite immature. Many of these youngsters get into trouble.

Many children who are not properly controlled and disciplined bring shame and disgrace on their fathers and mothers. In contrast, the wise man said:

Discipline [Correct, NEB] your son, and he will give you rest [he will be a comfort to you, NEB]; he will give delight to your heart (v. 17).

What about your children? Are they left to themselves to run wild, or are they properly controlled and disciplined? The undisciplined child not only may bring shame to his mother (and father); such a child is usually an unhappy child. Teenagers may at times rebel against parental authority, yet many of them really want parents to set some limits for them.

You do not lose your children by "calling the shots" for them. This is true as long as you do it in the spirit of love and concern, and the decision-making process is gradually shifted to the maturing son and/or daughter.

A Keeper of Vineyards
(Song of Sol. 1:6)

They made me keeper of the vineyards; but, my own vineyard I have not kept! (Song of Sol. 1:6).

An elderly teacher told about an incident in the life of a well-known preacher. He did not identify the preacher by name, but it was generally known to whom he referred. This man was a prominent pastor who became a well-recognized and highly-honored denominational leader. He had given himself unselfishly to the work of the church and denomination.

One of his sons had strayed far away from the preaching and teaching of his father. That son was at the point of death in his father's home. The father, according to the teacher, was pacing up and down the sidewalk in front of his home, wringing his hands and repeating over and over again, "Thou hast 'made me the keeper of the vineyards; but mine own vineyard have I not kept.'" He was condemning himself because he had neglected his own son while he was ministering to the sons of others. How tragic!

This tragedy comes to many homes, not only the homes of preachers and denominational workers, but the homes of Sunday School teachers and other church leaders.

Let us all be careful that we do not neglect our own vineyard. If we do not, we will be more effective in caring for the vineyards of others.

"Vain Offerings"
(Isa. 1:13)

Bring no more vain [meaningless, NIV; worthless, NASB] offerings;

....

I cannot endure [bear, NIV]
iniquity and solemn assembly (Isa. 1:13).

What a challenge to Israel in this first chapter of Isaiah by "the prince of the prophets"! Among other things, God, speaking to and through the prophet, declared that when they "spread our [their] hands in prayer" (v. 15, NIV), He would not see their hands or hear their prayers.

Why did God refuse to accept their worship, calling it worthless, or to hear their prayers? He said, "Your hands are full of blood" (NIV).

Then Isaiah, speaking for God, told them what they could and must do for them and their worship to be acceptable. His requirements are stated in several brief, pointed statements in verses 16-17. Then, typical of the prophets, he added, "Defend the fatherless, plead for the widows."

Let us never forget that the God revealed by the prophets and Jesus always had a special concern about the underprivileged. This, as well as other emphases of the great eighth-century prophets, is needed by contemporary Christians.

Our Heavenly Father is more interested in our treatment of our fellow human beings, particularly the neglected ones, than He is of the exactness or beauty of our worship services.

Our worship of the righteous, compassionate God can and will be vain, meaningless (NIV), or useless (NEB) if we are not right in our relations to our fellow human beings.

A Vision of God
(Isa. 6:5)

Woe is me! For I am lost; for I am a man of unclean lips, and I dwell in the midst of a people of unclean lips; for my eyes have seen the King, the Lord of hosts! (Isa. 6:5).

The Bible records visions of some of God's great servants: Moses at the burning bush, Isaiah, Samuel as a lad in the Temple, Peter on the housetop, and Paul on the Damascus Road.

The vision of Isaiah has some distinctive elements. His vision came "In the year that King Uzziah died" (v. 1). Even in the dark days of the death of a good king, God gave a vision to His prophet. Isaiah "saw the Lord sitting upon a throne, high and lifted up." He heard the seraphim singing, possibly antiphonally.

The prophet's immediate reaction to his vision was "Woe is me!" The seraphim were singing, but his lips were unholy and unworthy to join in the singing.

Why this conviction concerning unclean lips? Isaiah gave the answer: "For my eyes have seen the King, the Lord of hosts!" This is the natural reaction of anyone who is conscious of being in the presence of the holy God. After the cleansing, Isaiah was ready to respond to the Lord's "Who will go for us?" (v. 8).

Every recorded vision in the Bible includes a vision of command: there was something to do about it. So it is with every new insight we have regarding the way and will of the Lord.

Cleansed Lips and Lives
(Isa. 6:7)

Behold, this has touched your lips; your guilt is taken away, and your sin forgiven (Isa. 6:7).

You may want to think of this and the preceding treasure as one. There is some duplication, but both emphases are needed.

How grateful we ought to be that a consciousness of the presence of the Lord, the holy One, not only brings to us a deep sense of sin, it also brings us into contact with the source of cleansing from sin. There can be no cleansing, however, without an awareness of sin in our lives. The "Woe is me!" (v. 5) precedes the "Lo" (KJV) or "Behold" or cleansing.

There naturally follows from the cleansing a word from the Lord, "Whom shall I send, and who will go for us" (v. 8)?

This experience of Isaiah suggests several truths:

(1) As previously suggested, cleansing must come before we are prepared to hear the command of the Lord.

(2) The purpose of God in the cleansing goes beyond the cleansing itself; so it is with each experience we have in and with the Lord, including our conversion. Each in some way is preparatory.

(3) Our lips are not ready to proclaim God's message until they and our lives have been touched by the fire that comes from His presence.

(4) When our lips have been touched and cleansed by that fire, then we are prepared and willing to respond to His call: "Here am I, send me."

A Strange Servant of God
(Jer. 43:10)

Behold, I will send and take Nebuchadrezzar the king of Babylon, my servant, and he will set his throne above these stones which I have hid (Jer. 43:10).

Nebuchadrezzar was an enemy of Israel, the people of God, and yet God referred to him as "my servant."

God used Nebuchadrezzar to punish His people who had been disobedient and disloyal to Him. I am sure that the children of Israel did not consider Nebuchadrezzar a "servant" of God.

It is even possible that Jeremiah, God's prophet, had some difficulty accepting the fact that Nebuchadrezzar was a servant of God to carry out His purposes. We do not believe that Nebuchadrezzar would have thought of himself as achieving God's purposes and, hence, being a servant of the Lord.

The fact that our Heavenly Father has used and still uses enemies of His people, and even His own enemies, to achieve His purposes underscores His greatness. That which was true in the days of Jeremiah may also be true in our own day.

We in America are not a chosen people such as was true of Israel, but we have been unusually favored by the Lord. Let us never forget, however, that our Heavenly Father may use a people we may consider our enemies, and even His enemies, to punish us for our unfaithfulness.

The God of the Nations
(Jer. 44:2)

You have seen all the evil that I brought upon Jerusalem and upon all the cities of Judah (Jer. 44:2).

God was not only the God of Jeremiah and the other prophets, He was also the God of Judah and Israel. His prophets were to deliver His message to the people. The latter, in turn, were accountable for the response they gave to the message.

It is also clearly evident in the Old Testament that God was not only the God of His chosen people, He was also the God of all the nations. He is the sovereign God of the universe, and that means that His concern is all-inclusive.

The Lord gave Jeremiah a message not only about Judah but also concerning or against Egypt (46:2*ff.*); Philistia (47:1 *ff.*); Moab (48:1 *ff.*); Ammon (49:1 *ff.*); Edom (49:7 *ff.*); Damascus (49:23 *ff.*); Babylon (50:1 *ff.*); (see Amos 1:3,6,9,11,13; 2:1,4,6).

It would be wise for us as contemporary Christians and Americans to remember that God is still the God of the nations. He not only holds individuals accountable, but nations also are accountable to Him. His judgment ultimately will come on any nation that opposes Him and His purposes in the world.

And we should remember that God is no respecter of nations as well as of persons. His own people Israel, as well as their enemies, were judged by Him, and we should not forget, as previously suggested, that God used other nations less righteous than Israel to punish His chosen people.

Responsibility of the Prophet
(Ezek. 2:7)

You shall speak my words to them, whether they hear [listen, NIV] or refuse to hear; for they are a rebellious house (Ezek. 2:7).

Those words of God to Ezekiel were and are His challenge to every spokesperson for Him. Remember that God also has some prophets today. The prophetic function is not restricted to pastors and preachers. There may be prophets in the pew as well as in the pulpit.

God's word to His prophets is the same for all generations. They have the responsibility to proclaim God's message. They should seek to be sure, however, that the message has come from the Lord.

Recognizing that the message is from the Lord, the prophet should and will deliver it unapologetically but with proper humility. The prophet is a mere instrument in the delivery of God's message.

Notice one other truth in God's instructions to His prophet—he was to deliver God's message, whether the people heard or refused to listen to it. The prophet's responsibility was and is the delivery of the message. What the hearers do about it was and is their responsibility.

This puts a heavy responsibility on the prophet of God whether in pew or pulpit. One should be sure that the message is from God. One should be equally certain that one delivers the message clearly and uncompromisingly, yet with concern and compassion.

Idols in the Heart
(Ezek. 14:3)

These men have taken their idols into their hearts (Ezek. 14:3).

This same expression, "idols in their hearts," is found in verses 4 and 7. Ezekiel, a prophet of the Exile, was addressing "the house of Israel" (v. 6). They had become "estranged" from God "through their idols" (v. 5).

An idol is something or someone that is made an object of worship. Anyone or anything, animate or inanimate, can become an idol. This is true if supreme value is attached to it.

For Israel, their idols were the false gods of the peoples among whom they had lived. These false gods could not save them. Truly, their worship of false gods caused their captivity.

It was to these idols that Israel had given their devotion. They had enshrined them in their hearts, giving them the devotion which should have been reserved for God.

We in our day may not worship the same kind of false gods as did the Israelites, but do we as a nation, as churches, and as individuals not worship false gods that we have enshrined in our hearts?

Let us not forget that anything to which we attach supreme value in our lives or to which we give our allegiance is our god. What false gods or idols do we have in our hearts: our family, our jobs, our prestige, our financial security, or our favorite form of recreation—football, golf, and so forth?

Even our church can become an idol in our hearts.

God's Nevertheless
(Ezek. 16:60)

Nevertheless, I will remember My covenant with you in the days of your youth, and I will establish an everlasting covenant with you (Ezek. 16:60, NASB).

The word *nevertheless* usually introduces something different from or even opposite to what has just been said or done. "Nevertheless" in this verse is preceded with the announcement of God's judgment.

Then, God speaking to and through the prophet promised that He would remember the covenant that He had made with His people previously. This may have referred to the covenant at Mount Sinai. Also, He said to the prophet that He would establish an everlasting covenant with them.

The idea of the covenant is as central and unifying as any idea or concept in the Scriptures. It is very prevalent in the Old Testament. In the New Testament, the concept of a new and better covenant is more or less prominent, particularly in the Book of Hebrews (see Heb. 7:22; 8:8,13; 9:15; 12:24).

How grateful we should be for the grace and goodness of God expressed in His "nevertheless." His grace was expressed not only in His dealings with Israel, it is also extended to other peoples, and to us as individuals.

When we disobey Him and sin, judgment inevitably comes, but it is followed with a "nevertheless" which reminds us that our original covenant with Him when we came into His family was and is a "Nevertheless" covenant.

Watchman for the Lord
(Ezek. 33:7)

So you, son of man, I have made a watchman for the house of Israel; whenever you hear a word from my mouth, you shall give them warning from me (Ezek. 33:7).

Ezekiel was a watchman for the Lord. Every prophet of God, ancient and contemporary, was and is a watchman. There is a sense in which every child of God should be a prophet, spokesman, or spokeswoman for the Lord and hence has a responsibility of being a watchman.

It is a watchman's responsibility to hear and proclaim the word the Lord gives to him for the people. If he is faithful in fulfilling this responsibility, he will not be held accountable for how the people respond to his message.

If the watchman fails to warn the people by proclaiming God's word, then he will be held accountable.

This is one of the potent passages in the Bible on personal responsibility. But it should never be forgotten that there is involved a two-way responsibility: the watchman, which really includes all of us who are children of God, and those who hear the watchman's word of warning.

How faithful are we as watchmen? How responsive have we been and are we as hearers?

The Youth—The Man
(Dan. 1:8; 6:10)

But Daniel purposed [resolved] in his heart that he would not defile himself. . . . Now when Daniel knew that the writing was signed, he went into his house; and in his windows being open in his chamber toward Jerusalem, . . . he kneeled upon his knees three times a day, and prayed (Dan. 1:8; 6:10, KJV).

One can frequently see the man in the boy or the youth. Daniel the young man had the strength of purpose to resist the rich foods and wine from the king's table. As a mature man he consistently prayed to his God in spite of the trap his enemies laid for him.

The leaders of the kingdom of Darius, jealous of Daniel, wanted something they could use as a charge against him. They paid Daniel a glowing compliment when they said: "We shall not find any ground for complaint against this Daniel unless we find it in connection with the law of his God" (6:5).

Appealing to the egotism of the king, they led him to agree that anyone who made "petition to any God or man for thirty days," except to the king, would be cast into the den of lions.

What was Daniel's response? Using the words that were applied to him as a young man, we could properly say, "But Daniel purposed [resolved] in his heart" that he would proceed with his usual periods of prayer and devotion.

The most thrilling part of this whole story is not the miraculous deliverance of Daniel from the lions but the courage of Daniel. This courage was typical of his life from youth to maturity.

"But if Not"
(Dan. 3:17-18)

Our God whom we serve is able to deliver us from the burning fiery furnace; and he will deliver us out of your hand, O king. But if not, be it known to you, O king, that we will not serve your gods or worship the golden image which you have set up (Dan. 3:17-18).

The "but if nots" of life frequently reveal the depths of one's conviction and the strength of one's character. The three young Hebrews believed that their God was able to deliver them, but even if He did not, they would not turn from worshiping Him to the gods of the king. They would give their lives rather than be unfaithful to their God and to their own inner convictions.

Do we have the but-if-not kind of courage? It is claimed that "honesty is the best policy," but what if it is not? What if honesty would cause us to lose the game? To flunk the examination? To be fired from the jobs? Reduce our profit or income? Would we still be honest?

We sing "It pays to serve Jesus," *but if not,* would we serve Him anyway? We believe our Heavenly Father can shield or at least deliver us and our loved ones from the burdens, pressures, and dangers of life. *But if not,* would we still retain our faith in Him and continue to trust His promises that have sustained and comforted us?

Gods of Gold
(Dan. 5:23)

You have praised the gods of silver and gold, of bronze, iron, wood, and stone, which do not see or hear or know, but the God in whose hand is your breath, . . . you have not honored (Dan. 5:23).

These words were a part of Daniel's message to Belshazzar, the son and successor of Nebuchadrezzar. Instead of praising the true God who had power over his life and death, he and they praised and worshiped gods of silver and gold.

There is no condemnation in the Scriptures of money and material things in general. Over and over again, however, the danger of material things is emphasized. The severest threat comes when the material is substituted for the spiritual—when gold displaces God.

The threat of the substitution of gold and material things for God and His worship and service is one that many of us as individual Christians constantly face. Material things can be a great blessing. They are a curse, however, when they are given supreme value in our lives.

Our churches also need to be on the alert for the threat of materialism; they, as is true of us as individuals, may worship gods of gold.

"Return to the Lord"
(Joel 2:13)

Return to the Lord, your God,
for he is gracious and merciful [compassionate, NIV; NEB],
slow to anger, and abounding in steadfast love [lovingkindness,
NASB] (Joel 2:13).

The prophet had painted a dark picture of the day of the Lord. It was to be a time of judgment upon His people. Then, beginning with verse 12, there is a call for repentance; "Return to the Lord, your

God." He was still their God even though they had strayed far away from Him, and His judgment was coming upon them.

The basis for the prophet's appeal was the fact that God was gracious, merciful or compassionate, slow to anger, and abounding in steadfast love.

It seems clear that our nation has drifted away from God and from many of the qualities that have made us great. There are threats to our nation from without but primarily from within. We need to hear the prophet's invitation: "Return."

Some of our churches may need to hear the words: "Return to the Lord." Some of them have become so enamored with buildings and prestige that they no longer minister to the real needs of people and hence no longer fulfill the purpose of God.

What about us as individual children of God? Do we need to hear the invitation or admonition to return to the Lord? Have we drifted away from our love for God and our devotion to Him and His cause? If so, we need to heed the invitation: "Return."

How glorious to remember that if we as a nation, a church, and as individuals return to the Lord He will receive, forgive, and bless us.

A "Therefore" of Judgment
(Amos 5:11)

> You trample on the poor
> and force him to give you grain.
> Therefore, though you have built
> stone mansions, you will not live in them;
> though you have planted lush
> vineyards, you will not drink their wine (Amos 5:11, NIV).

Some of the most important words in the Scriptures may seem to be rather insignificant. Some of them are conjunctives such as "therefore." As a conjunctive, "therefore" frequently ties together important ideas or concepts.

The word is prominent in both Testaments. In the Old Testament it is particularly prevalent in the writings of the prophets. For example, it is found ten times in Amos (3:2,11; 4:12; 5:11,13,16,27; 6:7;

7:16,17). In all of these references except one (5:13), it is a "therefore" of judgment.

Most Old Testament prophets lived during a critical time for their nation. They saw the impending judgment of God. They sought to help the leaders and the people to understand why God's judgment was coming. A major emphasis was upon the mistreatment of the poor and needy. In other words, the prophets of God were generally on the side of the underprivileged. For example, the verse in Amos following the one quoted above is:

> For I know how many are your offenses,
> and how great your sins.
> You oppress the righteous and take bribes
> and you deprive the poor of justice in the courts
> (NIV).

Contemporary prophets walk in the footsteps of the prophets of old; they will fearlessly proclaim the word they have received from the Lord. They will be God's spokespersons for and defender of the masses.

Fleeing from God
(Jonah 1:3)

> But Jonah rose to flee to Tarshish from the presence of the Lord. He went down to Joppa (Jon. 1:3).

Jonah was not the first or the last person to attempt to flee from the presence of God. You have doubtlessly heard preachers and others tell how they fought against the call of God. Some have seemed to elude Him and wander far into sin.

Most of us, at some time and for some reason, have attempted to flee from the presence of God. It could have been we were afraid of His presence because of some sin in our lives. We may have known that He wanted us to do something we were unwilling to do. Or we may have had some hurtful habit we knew God wanted us to give up.

Jonah discovered he could not escape the presence of God. He might board a ship bound for Tarshish, but God was on the ship with him. He might be thrown overboard into the sea, but God was there with him. God was even present with Jonah in the belly of the great fish. Jonah could not escape away from God. Many of us have discovered that wherever we flee, God is there.

How much better it would have been for Jonah to have accepted God's commission and been His willing agent in delivering His message to Nineveh. So it is with us. We cannot escape His presence: Why should we attempt to do so?

What the Law Requires
(Mic. 6:8)

What does the Lord require [asks, NEB] of you but to do justice, and to love kindness and to walk humbly with your God? (Mic. 6:8).

In the Bible there are several summaries of the basic requirements of our biblical faith. This is one of the greatest.

Micah gave a threefold answer to his question. First, "to do justice" applies to all of God's children in every relationship of life: employer-employee, teacher-student, parent-child, white-black, and so forth. God's children are to be just in all their dealings and in every relationship of life.

Second, Micah mentioned "to love kindness" or "mercy" (NIV). This involves kindness to all but possibly particularly to those who need it most: children, old people, the handicapped, and neglected.

The third element in this summary by Micah is "to walk humbly with your God." Would you agree that if we walk with Him we will be humble? The more closely we follow Him, the more conscious we will be that we are unworthy of His presence and blessing.

There was an Old Testament person who walked with God and was not, because God took him. A little girl expressed Enoch's walk as follows: "One day when Enoch was out walking with God, God said to him, 'It is closer to My home than it is to yours. Just come on home with Me.'"

May that be His word to you and me as we approach the end of the journey.

Light in Darkness
(Mic. 7:8)

> Rejoice not [do not gloat, NIV] over me, O my enemy;
> when I fall, I shall rise;
> when I sit in darkness,
> the Lord will be a light to me (Mic. 7:8).

Have you ever been reading the Bible and had a verse or a portion of a verse seem to jump out of the page at you? It may have been a familiar verse or one that you did not remember ever having read before. If you have had such an experience you know that the verse suddenly came to life because of some need in your life at that particular time.

I had such an experience several years ago. I was reading the Book of Micah in connection with the writing of some program material for young people. That day I was about as despondent and discouraged as I ever get. As I read, all of a sudden some words stood out from the page. I still remember where they were located in the Bible that I was reading. Those words spoke to my need that day and have repeatedly spoken to me since then. Few verses of Scripture have meant more to me through the years.

It was the latter part of Micah 7:8 that spoke and still speaks to me in a particular way: "When I sit in darkness,/the Lord will be a light to me." Whatever may be the reason for the darkness in your life and mine, the Lord will be a light unto us, if we will let Him. It seems at times that the darker the night the brighter the light that comes from His presence.

Cheating God
(Mal. 1:14)

Cursed be the cheat who has a male in his flock, and vows it, and yet sacrifices to the Lord what is blemished (Mal. 1:14).

We do not make animal sacrifices as was true of the Israelites, but there are many ways that we can cheat or swindle (NASB) the Lord. The prophet elsewhere reminded the people that they had cheated or robbed God in their "tithes and offerings" (3:8).

Are you and I cheating God? Have we and do we cheat Him by failing to give to His cause what we have pledged or what we should give?

Church staffs and leaders should recognize that churches can cheat God. They can fail to give what they pledge to the worldwide causes of Christ. They can withhold for themselves what should be given elsewhere. It is as wrong for a church to be too self-centered as it is for an individual child of God.

Furthermore, the prophets of God through the centuries have reminded His people that they have a responsibility to the poor and the underprivileged. We may deprive them of what God expects us to share with them.

Let us ask ourselves: "Are we cheaters?" And we can be cheaters not only regarding things material. We can cheat God and His church by failing to give the time and energy that should be given to the work of His kingdom.

"Follow Me"
(Matt. 4:19)

Follow me [come with me, NEB], and I will make you fishers of men
[I will teach you to catch men, GNB] (Matt. 4:19).

This was the invitation of Jesus to Peter and Andrew who were fishermen. The invitation was repeated to John and James (v. 21). There are two or three abidingly relevant truths in the invitation.

Jesus never asked anyone to go before Him. His continuing word was and is, "Come, follow Me."

He promised to use the skills of those early disciples. We can be assured that if we follow Him, He will use every talent and all the training we have received. We will discover maximum fulfillment as we respond to His invitation.

Responding to His call to follow Him will enable us to do some things that we could not do apart from Him. Those disciples were fishermen; He would enable them to become fishers of persons.

The indwelling Christ is still in the business of utilizing and multiplying talents and skills of those who will respond to His invitation. He offers to make us what we are not.

And let us never forget that His invitation is a continuing one: none of us ever follows Him perfectly. Have you heard or do you hear His invitation, "Come, follow me, and I will make you . . ."?

Sins of the Mind
(Matt. 5:28)

Every one who looks at a woman to lust for her has committed adultery with her already in his heart (Matt. 5:28, NASB).

This statement by Jesus should give to you and me a deepened sense of sin in our lives. Many of us may be relatively free from the grosser sins of the flesh, but what about the sins of the mind? We can sin with our minds but show no outward expression.

The look geferred to by Jesus was not a passing glance. It was to look "at a woman so as to have an evil desire for her" (Williams) That "evil desire" was the lust to commit adultery with her. There might be many reasons why one would not actually commit adultery, but if the desire is there, it is sin. There can be psychological as well as physical adultery.

The same may be true of other sins. For example, there may be the temptation to lose our tempers, to curse, to tell a dirty story, to drink, and so forth. But for various reasons the temptation may be resisted, yet the desire lingers on. If the latter is true, then it, like adultery, becomes a sin of the mind.

What Christian would dare to say that he or she is completely free from sins of the mind?

Will you not agree that an appropriate daily prayer for us would be the words of the psalmist:

Let the words of my mouth and the meditation of my heart be acceptable in thy sight, O Lord, my rock and my redeemer (Ps. 19:14).

The Forgiving and the Forgiven
(Matt. 6:14-15)

> For if you forgive men their trespasses [wrongs, NEB], your heavenly Father also will forgive you; but if you do not forgive men their trespasses, neither will your Father forgive your trespasses (Matt. 6:14-15).

These words follow immediately the Model Prayer. One petition in that prayer was, "Forgive us the wrong we have done, as we have forgiven those who have wronged us" (NEB). This is the only petition about which Jesus speaks.

His comments plainly suggest that the forgiveness of our Heavenly Father is related to and dependent upon our forgiveness of those who have wronged us or sinned against us.

It sounds paradoxical, but God's forgiveness depends on our forgiveness of others. We are moved to forgive others because of His forgiveness of us. Paul's words apply to all Christians: "As Christ forgave you, so you must also forgive" (Col. 3:13). It should encourage us to forgive others if we remember that God, the Perfect One, has had to forgive more in us than we will ever have to forgive in others.

To sum up: the forgiving sinner will be forgiven. Also, the forgiven sinner should be the *forgiving* sinner.

God or Money
(Matt. 6:24)

You cannot be slaves of God and money (Matt. 6:24, Williams).

These words climax the fullest statement in the New Testament concerning the followers of Christ and material possessions. Jesus had taught that a disciple of His should concentrate on heavenly rather than earthly riches. He had pointedly said that "No one can be a slave to two masters" (Williams). Then he gave the reason this was true: "He will hate one and love the other, or else he will be devoted to one and despise the other" (Williams).

We should notice that Jesus did not say, "You *should not* serve or be a slave of God and money"; He said, "You *cannot*" (author's italics). Just as it is impossible for a slave to belong to and serve two masters, so it is impossible to be a servant or slave of both God and of money.

Many Christians through the centuries have tried to prove that Jesus was wrong. They have sought to serve both God, money, and the things that money will buy. Are you and I among those who profess to belong to Christ and at the same time are mastered by money and material things?

One thing is sure: in so far as we are slaves of money and the material, we do not serve God. Holding onto material things weakens our grip on God and spiritual things.

The way we can keep from being mastered by money is to let the Master master us. The indwelling Christ can enable us to make money a servant or a slave rather than a master.

The Compassionate Christ
(Matt. 9:36)

When he saw the crowds, he had compassion for them, because they were harassed [distressed, NASB] and helpless [downcast, NASB], like sheep without a shepherd (Matt. 9:36).

Here are two or three challenging truths concerning the compassion of Christ.

His compassion was individualized as well as generalized. He had compassion on the crowds or multitude, but He also had compassion on the widow of Nain and brought her son back to life (Luke 7:11-17), on two blind men and opened their eyes (Matt. 20:30-34), on the leper and healed him (Mark 1:40-42).

We will find also, if we study the record carefully, that Jesus reached out in compassion to all kinds of people. His compassion was not selective.

Furthermore, His compassion was not compartmentalized. He had concern for the total person, for the body as well as the soul.

Still another great truth concerning the compassion of Christ was that He did something about it. His compassion was not a vapory sentimentality.

How much of His compassion finds expression in and through our lives? Do we have a compassion for the multitudes? But also, do we have a compassion for the individuals whose lives we touch? Do we reach out in compassion to minister to the physical and emotional needs of people as well as their spiritual needs? Do we do something tangible to express our compassion?

Come for Comfort
(Matt. 11:28)

Come to me, all of you who are tired from carrying heavy loads, and I will give you rest (Matt. 11:28, GNB).

We should be grateful for the three Synoptic Gospels. Each makes some distinctive contributions to our knowledge of what Jesus did and taught. This verse and its context is one of Matthew's contributions that has meant a great deal to God's children through the centuries.

It is possible that the immediate reference of Jesus was to burdens or the heavy load of the law. The scribes and Pharisees applied the law to such minute details in life that it had become a burden to the people.

It is possible, however, that Jesus here referred to loads or burdens of any kind. He may have had in mind the actual heavy physical burdens that many had to carry in those days and still have to carry in some places in the world.

Whatever may be the nature of our burdens, He promises to give us rest or relief (NEB).

How does He give relief? There may be occasions when the actual burden itself is removed. But the experience of many of us is that many times the burden remains. We can be grateful, however, that He gets under the load or burden with us. When He is there, the burden becomes lighter.

After all, the apostle Paul did not have his thorn in the flesh removed, but God did say to him, "My grace is sufficient for you" (2 Cor. 12:9). We will find His grace sufficient, whatever may be the burdens that come in life.

Hardness of Heart
(Matt. 19:8)

He said to them, "For your hardness of heart Moses allowed [permitted, NASB] you to divorce your wives, but from the beginning it was not so" (Matt. 19:8).

Jesus had stated it was the purpose of God for one man and one woman to be joined together as husband and wife for life. The Pharisees pressed Him with an additional question: "Why then did Moses command one to give a certificate of divorce, and to put her away." (See Deut. 24:1-4.)

Notice the reply of Jesus. He replied that Moses *allowed* or *permitted* them. Jesus also gave the reason for the permission: "For your hardness of heart." The responsibility for the permission rested on the people rather than on Moses.

This conversation of Jesus with the Pharisees should help us understand some questions regarding certain moral problems of the Old Testament. Some things in the Old Testament seem out of harmony with the spirit and teachings of the New Testament. Jesus plainly indicated that the provision for divorce in the law was by permission. It was not a part of God's original purpose or of His ultimate will.

Since this is true regarding divorce, it may also be true of other matters in the Old Testament. The full and perfect revelation of God was in and through Jesus. This means that the Old Testament is to be read and particularly to be evaluated in light of the New Testament. The latter is to be normative for the child of God.

The Second Commandment
(Matt. 22:39)

And a second is like it, You shall love your neighbor as yourself (Matt. 22:39).

Notice that love of neighbor is not "the great and first commandment" (v. 38); it is "second." When right relations to God and people are found together, as in the Ten Commandments, the former is stated first. There should never be any question about which is "*the* great commandment in the law" (v. 36, author's italics).

The lawyer had only asked Jesus regarding *the* great commandment. Why did Jesus add, possibly after a pause for emphasis, "a second is like it"? Jesus may have meant that the second was like the first in motive; both were commandments of love.

It is also possible that Jesus meant that the second was like the first in importance. They belonged together; one was incomplete without the other. No one can love a neighbor as self who does not love God supremely. On the other hand, one who loves God will love one's neighbor, and we should remember that "neighbor" is an all-inclusive term. Plainspoken John said, "If anyone says, 'I love God,' and hates his brother, he is a liar" (1 John 4:20).

And let us never forget that Jesus, in the parable of the good Samaritan (Luke 10:29-37) and elsewhere, clearly revealed that no limitations should ever be placed on "neighbor." Our neighbor is anyone who needs our love and ministry.

The Invitation of Jesus
(Mark 1:17)

Jesus said to them, "Come with me, and I will teach you to catch men" (Mark 1:17, GNB).

One of the most interesting and fruitful ways to study the Scriptures is to study more or less frequently used words. One such word is *come*.

The word of Jesus to Simon and Andrew was, "Come with me." This was and is His initial invitation to any man or woman. It is an invitation to discipleship.

On one occasion Jesus spoke of Himself as the Bread of life. He followed that statement by saying, "He who comes to me shall not hunger" (John 6:35). He also said, "If any one thirst, let him come to me and drink" (John 7:37). Are you hungry? Are you thirsty? Is there a sense of something lacking in your life? If so, the word of Jesus is, "Come, satisfy your hunger and your thirst."

Then there is that wonderful invitation: "Come to me, all who labor and are heavy laden, and I will give you rest" (Matt. 11:28). As was true of most of Jesus' invitations, this was universal. It was addressed to the multitude. He said to them, and would say to us, "Others may promise you rest or relief; I will give it."

And let us never forget those wonderful words of Jesus: "Him who comes to me I will not cast out" or "I will never turn away anyone who comes to me" (John 6:37, GNB). Whatever may be the reasons for which we come to Him, He will never turn us aside!

Touch of Compassion
(Mark 1:41)

And Jesus, moved with compassion, put forth his hand, and touched him, and saith unto him, "I will, be thou clean (Mark 1:41, KJV).

This one touched by Jesus was a leper. Lepers in those days were avoided. Jesus never let anything, except the people's lack of faith, keep Him from ministering to their needs. This was not only true of the leper and those with other physical ailments; it was also true of social and moral outcasts in general. Those who reached up to Him for help felt His healing touch on their lives.

The secret to the fact that Jesus touched even the leper was His compassion (see treasure 60, Matt. 9:36). His compassion was not merely an emotion. It moved Him to do something about it. He had compassion on the multitude and fed them (Matt. 15:32); on two blind men, touched their eyes, and healed them (Matt. 20:30-34); on the widow of Nain, "touched the bier," and brought her son back to life (Luke 7:11-15). How grateful we ought to be for the compassion of Christ and for the touch that accompanied and expressed that compassion.

One test of our compassion for people is our willingness to reach out and touch those in need. We cannot be effective channels for the compassion of Christ unless we are willing to become involved in seeking to meet the needs of people. There is no substitute in human relations for the touch of a hand motivated by a compassionate heart.

Sabbath Made for Mankind
(Mark 2:27)

The sabbath was made for man, not man for the sabbath (Mark 2:27).

A chief point of controversy of Jesus with the Pharisees was regarding the sabbath. They had made the sabbath a burden to the people.

He enunciated at least three important principles regarding the sabbath: (1) It was "lawful to do good on the sabbath" (Matt. 12:12). (2) He was the Lord of the sabbath (Luke 6:5). (3) "The Sabbath was made for the good of man" (Mark 2:27, GNB). The last suggests that the God who created us knows what is good for us. The same general principle applies to every provision that God has made for human beings: they are "for the good of man."

This means that God's basic laws are not the arbitrary requirements of some oriental despot. They are in harmony with human nature. God's laws, including the Ten Commandments, are not primarily to limit us but to release us.

Properly understood, we will see that God's laws or commandments are not grievous or burdensome (1 John 5:3). Just as a giant locomotive finds its freedom and fulfills its purpose by staying on its tracks, so we will find our greatest freedom when we conform to the laws and purposes that God has provided. They restrain, but it is a restraint that brings a maximum of freedom.

Faith and Fear
(Mark 4:40)

He said to them, "Why are you afraid? Have you no faith?" (Mark 4:40).

The disciples were crossing the Sea of Galilee. They were caught in "a great storm of wind" (v. 37). Jesus was asleep in the stern of the boat. The disciples woke Him and asked Him, "Teacher, do you not care if we perish?" (v. 38).

He arose, rebuked the wind, and said to the sea, "Peace! be still!" (v. 39). Where there had been a great storm there was now a great calm.

Then He turned to the disciples and asked them, "Why are you afraid? Have you no faith?" Fear and faith do not belong together. Fear is a sign of a lack of faith. After all, Jesus was in the boat with them.

We do not row a boat across the Sea of Galilee, but we frequently find ourselves in the midst of the storms of life. One thing we should always remember when storms arise: if we are children of God, the Christ who stilled the storm on Galilee is in the boat with us. This should give us the peace that passes understanding. He may or may not still the storm, but we can be assured that in the midst of the storm He will be with us.

In other words, He may not in some miraculous way still the storms of life, but if we will let Him, He will work a greater miracle by giving us peace in the midst of storms. The quietness will make us a greater blessing as we touch others who are in the midst of the storms of life.

The Wind Ceased
(Mark 6:51)

He got into the boat with them and the winds ceased (Mark 6:51).

The disciples were having difficulty rowing their boat "for the wind was against them." Sometime "between three and six o'clock in the morning, he came to them, walking on the water" (v. 48, GNB). They thought He was a ghost and were afraid. He said to them, "It is I. Don't be afraid!" (v. 50, GNB). Then He got into the boat, and the record says the wind ceased.

What about the winds we have to buck in our lives? If we let Him step into the boat, will the winds cease? It depends on what we mean when we say "the winds ceased." Some winds do not cease; we continue in the midst of the storms. But what about the inner storm or disturbance? What about fear of the storms? When the Lord is in the boat with us, we can have inner calm in the midst of the storms of life. And let us never forget that He will be in the boat with us if we will invite Him in.

There is a grand old song many of us would list among our favorites. That song contains a statement, however, not in harmony with experiences that many of us have had. The words of the song are: "Take your burden to the Lord and leave it there." No, we cannot leave it. Most of the time He does not remove the burdens or eliminate the storms, but thank the Lord, He is in the boat with us, and when He is there, we need not be afraid of the storms, however severe they may be.

"And Peter"
(Mark 16:7)

> But go, tell his disciples and Peter that he is going before you to Galilee; there you will see him, as he told you (Mark 16:7).

These words of the angel at the empty tomb were spoken to the three women who early Sunday morning had brought spices to anoint the body of Jesus. The angelic being—or young man—delivered a message to the women from the resurrected Christ.

They were to remind the disciples of His plan, revealed to them previously, to meet them in Galilee. How forgiving, kind, and thoughtful of the risen Christ to add a special word: "and Peter."

Why the special word concerning Peter? Why was not the general word to the disciples sufficient? The additional "and Peter" was not because of the latter's importance. It is true that he had been the leader of the twelve. His name is always first in the listing of the apostles. Also, he was frequently the spokesman for them.

In recent days, however, he had not been acting like their leader. He had denied his Lord three times, underscoring his denial with oaths. Peter needed that "and Peter." He needed to know that his Lord had forgiven him.

The other disciples also needed to know that Peter was forgiven and restored. Also, it was important for Peter to meet the resurrected Christ in Galilee. It was on the shores of the Sea of Galilee that He searched the heart of Peter with His probing question: "Do you love Me?" repeated three times (John 21:15-17), which could not help but remind Peter that he had denied his Lord three times.

Regular Religious Habits
(Luke 4:16)

He came to Nazareth, where he had been brought up; and he went to the synagogue, as his custom was [as he regularly did, NEB] (Luke 4:16).

Jesus was no religious dropout. Although He was in frequent conflict with the religious leaders of His people, He did not permit this to keep him away from the regular place of worship. He went "as his custom was." Such attendance was a fixed pattern in His life.

This statement about Jesus should speak a searching word to many of His followers. Too many of us drop out when we see real or imagined faults or failures in our churches.

There are many excuses by church members for not attending the services of the church. They do not agree with the pastor; they do not like some of the people in the church; they have sick or elderly members of the family they need to visit; a husband or wife will not attend, and the spouse stays home with him or her; or they don't feel well: some church members have recurring weekend illnesses.

If we are inclined to give excuses for not attending, let us remember that Jesus went to the synagogue "regularly" or "as his custom was." Regular attendance should become as much a fixed pattern in our lives as it is for us to go to work or to school on Monday.

Jesus' Announcement of His Messiahship
(Luke 4:18-19)

The Spirit of the Lord is upon me,
because he has anointed me to preach [announce, NEB] good news
to the poor. He has sent me to proclaim release to the captives
and recovering of sight to the blind,
to set at liberty those who are oppressed [downtrodden, NASB],
to proclaim the acceptable [favorable, NASB] year of the Lord
(Luke 4:18-19).

When Jesus stood up in the synagogue of Nazareth to read the Scriptures, He was handed the book or scroll of Isaiah. The record says, "He opened the book and found the place where it was written"

(v. 17). Jesus never did anything by accident. Can you visualize Him turning the scroll until He found Isaiah 61:1-2?

After reading the Scripture, Jesus sat down and said to those in the synagogue, "Today this scripture has been fulfilled in your hearing" (v. 21). The coming of Jesus fulfilled Isaiah's words. This passage from Isaiah described the kind of Messiah He had come to be.

The words from Isaiah possibly helped John the Baptist on one occasion to know that Jesus was the Messiah. John sent two of his disciples to ask Jesus if He was the Messiah. Jesus told the disciples to go and tell John what they had seen and heard while they were with Him: "the blind receive their sight, the lame walk, . . . the poor have good news preached to them" (Luke 7:22).

When the two disciples reported to John the Baptist what they had seen and heard, I am sure his mind went back to Isaiah 61:1-2. This satisfied him. If that was what Jesus was doing, then He was the promised Messiah.

Peter's "Nevertheless"
(Luke 5:5)

And Simon answering said unto him, "Master, we have toiled all the night and have taken nothing; nevertheless at thy word [But because you say so, NIV] I will let down the nets" (Luke 5:5, KJV).

There are many incidents in the Scriptures that reveal the perspective of "nevertheless." One striking example is when God told Abraham to offer Isaac as a burnt offering. It is easy to imagine that Abraham might have said to the Lord: "Surely You do not want me to offer up Isaac, the child of promise. How can You fulfill Your purpose to bless the nations through my family if I offer him in sacrifice?" Then, I can imagine Abraham saying, "Nevertheless, at Your command I will do it." God always responds to that.

When Peter and his fishing partners, in response to Jesus' suggestion, cast their nets on the other side, they caught so many fish that their nets were breaking. They had to call for their partners to help. Their "nevertheless" paid rich dividends.

Have you known of individuals who have had a call of God that seemed unrealistic? A young man with a serious speech impediment felt called to preach. Many thought he was mistaken about the call of God. How could he ever preach?

However, the young man with a "nevertheless" kind of faith responded to God's call. He became a successful pastor, a seminary teacher, and ultimately head of a denominational agency.

How much of the "nevertheless" faith or perspective do you and I have?

"Andrew His Brother"
(Luke 6:13-14)

When it was day, he called his disciples, and chose from them twelve, whom he named apostles; Simon, whom he named Peter, and Andrew his brother (Luke 6:13-14).

Are you known primarily as someone's brother, son, or father. If so, then you can appreciate the problem that Andrew may have had. He was usually referred to as Simon's brother.

If any one of the twelve could justifiably have been jealous, it was Andrew. He was not included in the inner circle of the disciples along with his brother and his friends James and John. There were occasions when Jesus took along only these three. Why was Andrew left out? There is no way for us to know.

Really, if we did not have John's Gospel we would not know much about Andrew except that he was Simon's brother. John alone told us that Andrew brought his brother Simon to Jesus (John 1:40-42), that he told Jesus about the lad with the five barley loaves and three fish (John 6:8-9), and that with Philip he brought the Greeks to Jesus (John 12:29-22).

Andrew may have been best known as the brother of Simon, but that did not keep him from bringing people to Jesus, even his brother. Can you visualize Andrew back in the crowd on the day of Pentecost? Do you suppose the thought came to him as Peter preached, "Thank You, Father, I introduced him to Jesus"?

The Touch That Healed
(Luke 8:43-44)

A woman who had had a flow of blood [severe bleeding, GNB] for twelve years . . . came up behind him, and touched the fringe of his garment [the edge of his cloak, GNB]; and immediately her flow of blood ceased (Luke 8:43-44).

Wouldn't it be interesting to know why the woman was there and the source of her faith or hope as she reached out to touch the Master? Did she know someone who had been healed by Him? Did she have a loved one or a friend who knew Jesus personally and who had encouraged her to seek His help?

There is no way to know for sure what had encouraged her to be there. But can you visualize her in the crowd? She persistently pressed through the crowd until she could reach out, possibly rather timidly, and touch Jesus. When she touched just the fringe of His outer garment, wonder of wonders, she was healed!

Jesus asked, "Who was it that touched me?" (v. 45). He was being pressed and hence touched on every side. How did He know that she had touched Him? He gave the answer: "Some one touched me; for I perceive that power has gone forth from me" (v. 46).

We cannot in faith touch Jesus without being blessed. We cannot touch others for Him to bless them without paying a price for it. Power will go from us when we minister to them, but His power will in turn flow into our lives to resupply the strength and power that we have given in service to others for Him.

The More Important Question
(Luke 10:29, 36)

"Who is my neighbor?" . . . "Which . . . proved neighbor to the man who fell among the robbers?" (Luke 10:29,36).

You recognize that these questions are related to the story or the parable of the good Samaritan. The lawyer had given the summary of the law as supreme love for God and love for neighbor. Jesus had said, "Do this, and you will live" (v. 28). Then the lawyer asked, "And who is my neighbor?" Many Jews in the days of Jesus restricted "neighbor" to a fellow Jew.

Jesus, the matchless Teacher, made no attempt to answer directly the lawyer's question. Rather, as He so frequently did, He told a story or parable.

The lawyer wanted Jesus to place a limit on "neighbor" and hence on love, but Jesus never built any fences around any of His basic teachings. They were all limitless. If we derive any definition of "neighbor" from what Jesus said, it would have to be that our neighbor is anyone who is in need.

At the close of the story, Jesus asked the lawyer a far more important question than the one the lawyer had asked Him. The question of Jesus was: "Which . . . proved neighbor to the man who fell among the robbers?" (v. 36).

It is much more important for us to be a good neighbor than to know who is our neighbor.

At the Feet of Jesus
(Luke 10:39)

[Martha] had a sister called Mary, who sat at the Lord's feet and listened to his teaching (Luke 10:39).

The Gospels record three occasions when Mary, the sister of Lazarus and Martha, was in the presence of Jesus. Each time she was at His feet.

On this occasion she was sitting at His feet listening to the marvelous words that fell from His lips. What a privilege!

Later, her brother Lazarus became seriously ill, and his sisters sent word to their good friend, Jesus. You remember Jesus delayed His return until Lazarus had died. Martha went out to meet Him. He reasoned with her concerning the resurrection. Mary went out to greet Him and "fell at his feet" (John 11:32). Here she was at His feet with her sorrow. And how wonderful that the tender, sympathizing Jesus wept with her (John 11:35)!

The other occasion when we find Mary in the presence of Jesus was at the supper or banquet some of His friends gave for Him. His three close friends from Bethany were there: Lazarus at the table, Martha serving, and Mary again at His feet. This time she anointed His feet and wiped them with her hair (John 12:1-3). She had been taught by Him, she had taken her sorrow to Him, now she offered Him her devotion and worship.

Will you not agree that every one of us, men and women, who have been touched and blessed by Him should fall at His feet in gratitude for what He has done for us?

The Lament of Jesus over Jerusalem
(Luke 13:34)

O Jerusalem, Jerusalem, . . . How often would I have gathered your children tbgether as a hen gathers her brood under her wings, and you would not! (Luke 13:34)!

This heart cry of Jesus becomes very vivid for those of us who live or have lived on the farm. Can you see the mother hen with her wings spread over her chicks?

Under the mother hen the chicks are protected from the cold and from danger. If any danger is sensed by the hen, the chicks respond quickly to her warning signal. But Jerusalem did not heed the warning call of Jesus.

One wonders if Jesus would not address the same kind of call to contemporary cities. His word could be: "O Atlanta, O Birmingham, O Chicago, O Dallas, O Houston, how often would I have gathered your children together . . . but you would not." Some of the children may have heard His warning, but the vast majority did not and have not.

Let us look at the verse from another perspective. How much of the concern of Jesus do we have for the cities and for the people in those cities? E. Stanley Jones once said, "I wish my arms were long enough to put them around every person in the world." Do we have that kind of concern and compassion for people? If we do, it comes from the presence of the living Christ in our hearts who Himself wept over Jerusalem.

The Compassionate Father
(Luke 15:20)

He arose and came to his father. But while he was yet at a distance [a long way off, NEB], his father saw him and had compassion, and ran and embraced him and kissed him (Luke 15:20).

You recognize that this verse is a part of the parable of the prodigal son. The parable could just as properly be called the parable of the compassionate father.

The parable is preceded with the parables of the lost sheep and the lost coin. In both of these parables, that which was lost belonged to the one who was seeking for them.

So it was and is with the prodigal or lost son. He belonged to the father. Although the latter might not have been out seeking for him, he was on the alert for his return.

The main thrust of the parable is that the father, who had never ceased loving his son and looking for him to return, received him with open arms and heart.

How much this is like many a Christian father and mother who have seen a son or daughter stray away from the basic teachings of the home. Regardless of how far they have strayed away, they will be welcomed back.

The preceding will not be true of all fathers and mothers. It will be true of those who have felt the compassionate touch of the Heavenly Father as He has forgiven and welcomed us into His family.

God's and Caesar's
(Luke 20:25)

He said to them, "Then render to Caesar the things that are Caesar's, and to God the things that are God's" (Luke 20:25).

You remember the background for this statement by Jesus. The priests and scribes were seeking to trap Him. They sent spies to try to find something that could be used as a basis for an accusation against Him. They asked him, "Is it lawful for us to give tribute to Caesar, or not?" (v. 22). They evidently believed that whatever answer He gave would mean trouble for Him. If He said no He would be in trouble with Caesar; if He said yes He would be in trouble with the people.

Jesus asked for a coin. Possibly holding it up for all to see, He asked, "Whose face and name are these on it." (GNB). They replied, "Caesar's" or "the Emperor's" (GNB). He said, "Render to Caesar . . ." No wonder they "kept quiet, amazed at his answer" (GNB).

A perplexing question for Christians through the centuries has been, "What belongs to Caesar or the government, and what belongs to God?" There are at least four things, according to the Scriptures, that belong to Caesar: (1) Taxes—this is the only thing specifically taught by Jesus in this incident (see Rom. 13:7); (2) obedience (Rom. 13:1-5; 1 Pet. 2:13 *ff.*); (3) honor or respect (1 Pet. 2:17); and (4) intercessory prayer (1 Tim. 2:1-4).

On the other hand, what belongs to God? (1) We as individuals: the image of God is stamped upon us, and furthermore, we have been bought with a price (1 Cor. 6:19-20); (2) our supreme allegiance (Acts 4:18-20; 5:29); and (3) Caesar or the government as such (Rom. 13:1; John 19:9-11).

Stay: Testify
(Luke 24:29; Acts 1:8)

Stay in the city, until you are clothed with power from on high (Luke 24:49).

And you shall be my witnesses in Jerusalem and in all Judaea and Samaria, and to the end of the earth (Acts 1:8).

"Stay"; "You shall be witnesses." This is Luke's form of the Great Commission (see Matt. 28:18-20). We need in our lives as individual Christians and in our churches a balance between tarrying and witnessing or testifying.

Some children of God emphasize the staying so much they do little to share the good news of the gospel. They would like to remain on the mount of transfiguration and stay away from the world and its problems.

Others are so involved in the "work of the Lord" they do not take time to stay until the power comes. This explains the ineffectiveness of much that such Christians do or attempt to do for the Lord.

We need to cultivate the art of staying in the presence of the Lord. We should tarry expectantly and also obediently. The proper place in our lives for staying will enable us to witness more effectively not only by work or mouth but by the life we live.

Have we cultivated the capacity to stay until the power comes? Do we have the proper balancing in our lives of staying and witnessing or testifying?

Christ Changes Persons
(John 1:42)

Jesus looked at him and said, "Your name is Simon son of John, but you will be called Cephas." (This is the same as Peter and means "a rock," John 1:42, GNB).

When Andrew met Jesus, his immediate desire evidently was to bring his brother Simon to Jesus. To Simon, Jesus said, "Your name is . . . you will be." This is the word of Jesus to everyone who comes to Him.

Part of this change is immediate. In contrast, some phases of it represent a process. Some time after the initial visit of Simon to Jesus, the latter appeared on the shore of the Sea of Galilee. Simon and Andrew were casting a net into the sea. Jesus said to them, "Follow me, and I will make you fishers of men" (Matt. 4:19). And the Scripture says, "Immediately they left their nets and followed him" (v. 20). The direction of their lives was changed.

The words of Jesus, when Simon was introduced to Him, referred to a change so basic that it would justify a change in name. That change was not instantaneous for Simon. Such a change was for him as it is for us—a process. Simon did not look much like a rock during the arrest and trial of Jesus. On the day of Pentecost and the days following, he revealed more of the character of Peter the rock.

Can we hear the resurrected Christ say to us, "Your name is . . . you will be"? I believe He would say that to all of us: the most mature as well as the least mature. He is still in the process of changing people. We all need changing. We need to become more what He wants us to be. The main thing we can do to be changed is increasingly to let Him live in us and work out His will through us.

Spring of Living Water
(John 4:13-14)

Whoever drinks this water will get thirsty again, but whoever drinks the water that I will give him will never be thirsty again. The water that I will give him will become in him a spring which will provide him with life-giving water and give him eternal life (John 4:13-14, GNB).

This was a part of the conversation of Jesus with the Samaritan woman at Jacob's well. She had come to draw water.

Jesus, the matchless Teacher, related what He wanted to teach her to what she was doing. He contrasted the water she had come to draw to the water He could give. One who would drink the water she would draw would thirst again. Whoever drank of the water that He could give would never thirst.

Jesus explained that the water that He could give came from "an inner spring always welling up for eternal life" (NEB). This statement is graphic for those of us who live or have lived where there are springs. If you are one of those individuals, you can visualize the water bubbling up through the sandy bottom of the spring. Or, you see a never-failing stream of water coming out of the crevice in the rocks. The source of the spring is deep within the earth.

So it is with the life we have in Christ: a never-failing spring. In it there are resources to satisfy our spiritual thirst. However, the more mature we are in the Christian faith, the more we will recognize that while our thirst is satisfied when we partake of the living water, there is also a deepening thirst for a clearer understanding of and a closer walk with the One who is that Living Water.

God Is Spirit
(John 4:24)

God is spirit, and those who worship him must worship in spirit and truth (John 4:24).

This was another statement by Jesus to the Samaritan woman at the well. It has tremendous significance for us in our understanding of the worship of God and also how He works among human beings.

Since God is spirit, we must worship Him in spirit and in truth. One does not have to go to Jerusalem or Bethel to worship a God who is spirit. He can be worshiped anywhere.

It is important that His contemporary children attend regularly worship services of His and the church. They also should have a time for family worship.

However, since God is spirit, we can worship Him any place—in the car, at work, on the street, or at play, and so forth. If we sincerely reach out to Him, we can be sure that He will respond. He is spirit.

It may be wise to recognize that since He is spirit, His greatest miracles are spiritual rather than physical. He healed the paralyzed man, but a greater miracle was the forgiveness of his sin (Luke 5:18-26). He called and Lazarus came forth from the grave, but a greater miracle was when He changed a cursing, lying fisherman named Simon into Peter, the Rock, who preached on the day of Pentecost.

Paul prayed that his thorn in the flesh might be removed, but God worked a greater miracle by revealing to Paul that His grace was sufficient (2 Cor. 12:9).

Freedom in Christ
(John 8:36)

If the Son makes you free, you will be free indeed (John 8:36).

One of the most marvelous blessings that comes into our lives as a result of our union with the resurrected Christ is the freedom we have in Him. In the verse quoted above Jesus was speaking specifically of freedom from enslavement of sin. He had said, "Every one who commits sin is a slave of sin" (v. 34). One may be enslaved by a particular besetting sin, or one may be enslaved to sin in general. One can become a sin addict.

There are additional freedoms that come as a result of our union with Christ. These freedoms are closely related to and are dependent on our freedom from the enslavement of sin. One such freedom is freedom from fear. This may be fear of people in general or fear about what people will say and can do to us.

Then there is fear of the future. For young people this may be concern for—if not actual fear of—what the future holds: marriage, vocation, or career. For older people there may be a fear of old age and/or death. The Son can free us from these and other defeating fears.

Christ provides not only freedom *from* enslaving sin and defeating fears; He also provides freedom *for* some wonderful blessings: freedom for fellowship with Him, freedom to reach out to others for Him, and freedom to fulfill our potential for Him.

Sin and Suffering
(John 9:2)

His disciples asked him, "Rabbi, who sinned, this man or his parents, that he was born blind?" (John 9:2).

The relation of sin and suffering has been a perplexing problem for many Christians through the centuries. The generally accepted or orthodox position in the days of Jesus was that the two were directly related. This evidently was the perspective of the disciples. The man was born blind; they assumed that his blindness was punishment for sin—his or that of his parents.

This interpretation regarding the relation of sin and suffering is still prevalent. It may be defensible if sin is made broad enough to include sin in general, sin by society—its institutions and agencies—as well as sin by individuals.

But it is wrong to attribute all suffering to the sin of the sufferers and/or their families. The answer of Jesus to the disciples, which should be an answer to many of our questions regarding the source of suffering, was: "His blindness has nothing to do with his sins or his parents' sins. He is blind so that God's power might be seen at work in him" (GNB).

Really, the major question when suffering comes to us, a loved one, a friend, or a neighbor should not be: "Who sinned?" or "Why?" but rather "What?" or "How?" What does God want to do in and through the suffering? How will His power be seen at work in the one or those who suffer? What God is able to achieve through suffering will be determined by the reaction of those who suffer. May our prayer be that when suffering comes to us "that the works of God might be made manifest" in us.

The Basic Law of Life
(John 12:24)

Truly, truly, I say to you, unless a grain of wheat falls into the earth and dies, it remains alone; but if it dies, it bears much fruit (John 12:24).

Many of us were told in high school or college that self-preservation was the first law of life. Unquestionably, human beings have a strong desire to preserve life and to continue to live, but this Scripture reveals the most basic of all laws: the law of self-sacrifice, a law symbolized by the cross.

This law is written into the very nature of the universe. It is clearly basic in the physical world. New life comes by the literal or symbolic giving of life.

Jesus, on this particular occasion, applied this basic law to social and spiritual areas. He said, as He did on other occasions (see Matt. 10:38; 16:25): "He who loves his life loses it, and he who hates his life in this world will keep it for eternal life" (v. 25). Jesus also applied the basic law to His redemptive purpose: " 'I, when I am lifted up from the earth, will draw all men to myself.' He said this to show by what death he was to die" (vv. 32-33).

I believe that if we had truly spiritual eyes we would see a cross at the center of God's universe. The cross is much more than a symbol, even though it is the unifying symbol of our Christian faith. It expresses the basic law of God, a law that applies to all of life.

"A New Commandment"
(John 13:34)

A new commandment I give to you, that you love one another (John 13:34).

Jesus had frequently spoken of love previously. Why should He refer to love for one another as a new commandment?

There are two words sometimes translated "new." One means primarily young in contrast to aged or old. The other is "fresh" as opposed to "worn out." Here the latter word is used. There is something in the commandment that makes the old fresh: it is not worn out.

But in what way is this a new or fresh commandment? Possibly Jesus meant *new in its source*. Here He says, "I give to you." He was not quoting from the Old Testament as He did in the great summary of the Law (Matt. 22:34-40).

More importantly, the commandment was new in motive. We see this in the latter part of the verse: "As I have loved you, that you also love one another." In response to His love for them, they should love one another.

His commandment of love was also *new in its emphasis*. It commanded in a special way love for those in the Christian fellowship: "Love one another." As Christians we are to love all people but particularly and peculiarly we are to love fellow Christians.

Also notice that in "as I have loved you," there is not only motive and model but also standard or measure. How much did He love them? Enough that He was going to give His life for them. The measure of our love for one another is set by Christ's love for us.

"My Peace"
(John 14:27)

Peace I leave with you; my peace I give to you; not as the world gives do I give to you. Let not your hearts be troubled, neither let them be afraid (John 14:27).

This is from one of the closing chapters in John's Gospel, and it is not found in the other Gospels. These chapters record the closing conversations of Jesus with His disciples. We should be deeply grateful that John preserved them for us.

This particular chapter begins with those familiar words, "Let not your hearts be troubled." Jesus revealed to them that He was going to the Father's house and would there prepare a place for them.

He also told them that the Father would give them another Counselor, the Spirit of truth, who would dwell in them and be with them and teach them (15:26-27).

With that kind of background, Jesus said, "Peace is my parting gift to you, my own peace" (NEB). He was going away, but the peace that He gave would be a permanent possession of His disciples. It was not dependent upon His physical presence with them.

What a blessing it can be to all of us as God's children to know that through the indwelling resurrected Christ or the divine Spirit we can have His peace in the midst of the most difficult earthly circumstances. We can have that peace only if we are conscious of His indwelling presence.

"Apart from Him . . . In Him"
(John 15:5; Phil. 4:13)

Apart from me you can do nothing (John 15:5).
I can do all things in him who strengthens me (Phil. 4:13).

These two verses belong together. The first is in the memorable chapter where Jesus said He was the Vine, the disciples were the branches. The branches are an integral part of the vine. Their fruitfulness is dependent on the vitality of their relation to the vine. The lifeblood of the vine flows out through the branches.

As the branches bear fruit because of their connection with the vine, so it is with the disciples of Christ. He pointedly reminded them that without Him or apart from Him they could do nothing. In other words, their lives would be barren, void of fruit. So it will be with us, His contemporary disciples.

How grateful we ought to be, however, for the statement by Paul. It gives the other side of the picture. Apart from Christ and His presence we can do nothing, but because of our union with Him we can do all things. The "all things" includes anything that He wants us to do. We can do whatever is the will and purpose of God.

Because none of us maintains constantly as vital a relation to Him as we should, an additional word needs to be said. The fruit we bear for Him depends on how fully we let Him live in us and express Himself through us. The vitality of the relationship will determine whether the increase is thirty, sixty, or a hundredfold.

"So Send I You"
(John 20:21)

As the Father has sent me, even so I send you (John 20:21).

I never will forget when this statement of Jesus first really came alive for me. There are few verses that have challenged me more since that time. I started then to ask some questions that I have continued to ask since.

What did Jesus mean when He said, "So send I you"? He had a deep sense of having been sent. His disciples should have this same sense of having been sent. "Sent" is a key word in John's Gospel, being found more frequently than any of the three *L's: light, life, love* — which are so frequently associated with John's writings.

Jesus had a profound consciousness of having been sent to do the Father's will. He wants us to have a similar sense of having been sent—not to do our own will, but the will of the One who sends us.

What was the Father's will for Jesus? He came into the world to reveal God and to redeem humanity. We as His disciples are sent into the world to reveal Him and to be a redeeming influence among people. He was God incarnate, God in human flesh. He wants us to incarnate Him, so others can see Him in our lives. How clearly and fully do we reveal Him to others?

The conviction that He had been sent by the Father for a special mission gave Jesus a sense of holy urgency. He said, "We must work the works of him who sent Me as long it is day: night is coming when no man can work" (John 9:4, NASB). The deeper our conviction that He has sent us, the deeper will be our sense of "holy urgency."

"And Samaria"
(Acts 1:8)

You shall be my witnesses in Jerusalem and in all Judea and Samaria
and to the end of the earth (Acts 1:8).

Why did Jesus include "and Samaria"? Why not "and Galilee" or
"and Perea"? They were also close to Judea.

Jesus may have said "and Samaria" because of the prejudice of the
Jews against the Samaritans. They had "no dealings with Samaritans"
(John 4:9). It is said that the typical male Jew thanked God that he
was not born a slave, a woman, or a Samaritan. Jesus on numerous
occasions had revealed His attitude toward the Samaritans. For example, He talked to a Samaritan woman at Jacob's well, revealing to her
that He was the Messiah. He used a Samaritan as the hero of one of
His greatest parables.

The disciples to whom the commission was given were Jews and
had not gotten away from all their Jewish prejudices. The resurrected
Christ said to them that their witnessing should include the Samaritans—the people to whom it would be most difficult for many of them
to witness.

Most of us have our "and Samaria," some group or groups against
which we have strong prejudices. Is it the "down and outs" or the "up
and outs," those of a different nationality, another culture, or another
color? Whatever may be our "and Samaria" we should hear the words
of the risen Christ: "Don't neglect Samaria."

A Vision of Command
(Acts 9:6)

But arise and enter the city, and it shall be told you what you must do
(Acts 9:6, NASB).

The Bible contains some unusual visions of God. An examination
of those visions will reveal that they included a word of command.
God did not give a vision simply for its own sake. Paul's vision was
preparatory. There was a purpose in the vision that reached beyond
the vision itself.

This was true of Paul's experience on the Damascus Road. The Lord told him to go into Damascus, and there it would be revealed to him what he was to do. There was something for him to do about the vision.

We are not Elijahs, Samuels, Isaiahs, Pauls, or Peters, but somewhere along the way we have "met the Master" face-to-face. There was a purpose at work in that experience that went beyond the experience itself. There was something for us to do about it. When God saved me as a sixteen-year-old lad, I believe He knew then what He wanted me to do with my life for Him and for my fellow human beings.

The more we mature in the Christian life, the clearer we will understand that the major purpose of our initial experience was to start us on the way to fulfilling the purpose of God in our lives. We are to do something not only about the initial Christian experience but also about every subsequent experience we have with the Lord.

"Anything Unclean . . . Any Man Unclean"
(Acts 10:15,28)

Do not consider anything unclean [unholy, NASB; impure, NIV] that God has declared clean. . . . God has shown me that I must not consider any person ritually unclean or defiled (Acts 10:15,28, GNB).

These two verses from Acts 10 represent considerable progress on the part of Peter. On the housetop God had told the prejudiced Peter not to consider anything unclean that God had declared clean.

Peter was perplexed by the vision. In the house of Cornelius he saw more clearly what God was preparing him for on the housetop. It was a more or less natural but also a very difficult step for Peter from the housetop at Joppa to the house of Cornelius at Caesarea. Peter saw the lesson that God was seeking to teach him in and through the vision at Joppa. Now he understood that the vision was not primarily about clean and unclean animals but about "clean" and "unclean" people.

No wonder the first words of Peter when he started to speak were,

"I now realize that it is true that God treats everyone on the same basis (v. 34, GNB) or shows no partiality (see the next treasure). No one is "unclean" because of class, color, or condition of life.

Have we progressed far enough to hear the word of the Lord: Do not consider any person unclean?

Partiality
(Acts 10:34)

Peter opened his mouth and said: "Truly I perceive that God shows no partiality" (Acts 10:34).

In these, the opening words of Peter's sermon or message in the house of Cornelius, he said, "I perceive" that God shows no partality or "treats everyone on the same basis (GNB). Peter's statement implied progression in his comprehension of this great truth—"I now see" (NEB).

Part of the background for his understanding were the teachings of the Old Testament, with which he was doubtlessly well acquainted. Also, Peter had an opportunity to learn from the life and teachings of Jesus that God showed no partiality. He had seen Jesus associate freely with Samaritans, publicans, and sinners.

When we think of the opportunities that Peter had had to learn that God was no respecter of persons, it may seem that he was rather hard to convince. It took a vision from God to open his mind. He evidently did not fully grasp or at least admit the validity of this great truth until he stood in the presence of Cornelius, the Gentile, and those gathered together to hear his message.

Let us not be too hard on Peter, however, until we have grasped fully and applied more consistently in our own lives and in our churches the great truth that God is no respecter of persons or shows no partiality.

A Five-Word Biography
(Acts 10:38)

God anointed Jesus of Nazareth with the Holy Spirit and with power;
. . . he went about doing good and healing all that were oppressed by
the devil, for God was with him (Acts 10:38).

A lifetime of ministry and service is packed into the five words: "He
went about doing good." This five-word biography and a statement
made at the close of the visit of Jesus in the home of Zacchaeus, in
a sense, sum up the life of Jesus. The latter statement was, "For the
Son of man came to seek and to save the lost" (Luke 19:10).

Let us look more specifically at the five-word biography. First, it
implies that Jesus had a wayside ministry: "He went about." He did
not settle in one place and wait for the people to come to Him.

Had Peter spelled out more fully the content of "doing good," what
would he have included? He could have said, "He went about healing
the sick, feeding the hungry, comforting the sorrowing, forgiving the
sinful, and associating freely with all kinds of people."

What was the secret to the fact that Jesus went about doing good?
The good that He did flowed naturally and inevitably from within His
life. He had been anointed with the Holy Spirit and power, and "God
was with him."

Will people be able to say when we come to the end of the journey,
"[They] went about doing good"? This can and will be true to the
degree that we let the resurrected Christ live in us and express Himself
through us.

Singing at Midnight
(Acts 16:25)

About midnight Paul and Silas were praying and singing hymns to
God, and the prisoners were listening to them (Acts 16:25).

Some verses of the Bible, such as this one, are enriched if read in
their context. You may want to read or review verses 9-40.

You and I have not been beaten or cast into prison for our faith.
There are some Christians, however, even today who have had to
suffer for their faith.

Many of us have faced and do face midnights of loneliness and suffering. What have been our reactions? Have we been able to pray and to sing?

If we have prayed, what has been the nature of our prayers? What do you suppose Paul and Silas prayed for? Do you suppose they complained to God and asked, "Why?" Or do you think that they thanked God for considering them worthy to suffer for His cause? They may have prayed for the ones in prison with them, for the jailer and his family, as well as for their loved ones and friends.

At least their prayer seemed to have been naturally related to the singing of hymns. One does not sing praises to God from a critical heart or a defeated spirit.

What about our midnights of discouragement and suffering? Can and do we pray and praise the Lord when the darkness of midnight surrounds us?

What we let our midnights do to us will determine, to a considerable degree, what we can do for the One who walked farther into the garden of suffering than anyone else. The last few steps of that journey He had to take all alone.

One Human Race
(Acts 17:26)

From one man he created all races of mankind and made them live throughout the whole earth (Acts 17:26, GNB).

These words were a part of Paul's message to the proud Athenians. As Paul walked through their city he had observed an altar erected "To an unknown god." He declared unto them that this God, unknown to them, was the true God who "made the world and everything in it" (vv. 23-24). He was Lord of heaven and earth.

This same God "created all races of men." This was true of the proud Greeks and of the equally proud, self-conscious Jews. We are "of one" or "from one." Men and women of all races belong to one human race.

The attitude of any person or group of people cannot change the preceding fact. One may have a brother or a sister whose life-style one does not approve. This, however, does not change the relationship. Such a one is still a brother or a sister. So it is in the human family.

The same is also true in the Christian family. All of us who are Christians are of the family of God. We have the same Father regardless of color, culture, or condition of life. Our Father is impartial. We show our kinship to our Father by being impartial in our treatment of our brothers and sisters in Christ.

As human beings we have all descended from "one man" or "one forefather." As Christians we are one in Christ; we have one Father. We can sum up by saying, "We are one human race and one Christian family."

Obedient to the Heavenly Vision
(Acts 26:19)

Wherefore, O King Agrippa, I was not disobedient to the heavenly vision (Acts 26:19).

This was a part of Paul's defense before Agrippa. "Heavenly vision" referred to his experience on the Damascus Road when he was aware of the presence of the resurrected Christ. Included, however, was a revelation to him of the purpose of that vision.

The Lord said to Paul: "Rise and stand upon your feet; for I have appeared to you for this purpose, to appoint you to serve and bear witness to the things in which you have seen me and to those in which I will appear to you" (v. 16).

Notice the following, all of which are relevant for us: (1) "I have appeared to you for this purpose"—there was purpose in the appearance of the resurrected Christ to Paul; (2) the content of the purpose —"to serve and bear witness"; (3) the witnessing included not only the experience of Paul on the Damascus Road but also other things that would be revealed to him. The revelation of God's purpose for us, as for Paul, is a continuing experience. It was of this inclusive vision that Paul said he had not been disobedient.

We doubtlessly have not had a Damascus Road experience, but each of us has had his or her distinctive experiences with the resurrect-

ed Christ. The most searching question for us and for every child of
God is: Have we been obedient to the heavenly vision?

Teaching Ourselves
(Rom. 2:21)

You then who teach others, will you not teach yourself? (Rom. 2:21).

Here Paul was directing some pointed remarks to the Jews who
relied on the law and boasted of their relationship to God (v. 17). The
question that he asked in verse 21 was directed specifically to those
who taught others.

He asked some searching questions: "While you preach against
stealing, do you steal? You who say that one must not commit adultery, do you commit adultery? . . . You who boast in the law, do you
dishonor God by breaking the law?" (vv. 21-23).

The question for us in the contemporary period is: Do we practice
what we teach and preach? The greatest weakness of most of our
teaching and preaching is the fact that in our relations to others we
do not demonstrate as much as we should the teaching and preaching
that we do?

There are few things if any that will add more to the effectiveness
of what we say as teachers, preachers, or as Christians in general than
an honest, sincere effort to practice what we teach or preach.

An ounce of practice is worth a pound of proclamation. Most
people, particularly non-Christians, are not much impressed by what
Christians say unless they demonstrate in their lives something of the
spirit of Christ.

Newness of Life
(Rom. 6:4)

We were buried therefore with him by baptism into death, so that as
Christ was raised from the dead by the glory of the Father, we too
might walk in newness of life (Rom. 6:4).

Do you remember when and where you were baptized? I remember
my baptism quite well. I had been taught that baptism by immersion

symbolized the death, burial, and resurrection of Christ.

Later I came to understand that baptism also portrayed or pictured some important truths concerning the Christian's life. It symbolized the fact that one had died to the old life, had been buried with Christ, and had been raised to walk in newness of life.

What are some of the elements of this new life? There is or should be newness in attitude toward God, members of our family, our fellow human beings, and life in general. There should be newness in attitude toward the things that occupy our lives. Some things that formerly may have seemed important should now be considered insignificant. Also, things we once thought right to do we may now consider wrong or at least unwise.

There enters into the Christian's life also a newness of relationship: to God, to family, to the Christian fellowship, and to men and women in general.

There is at least one other important aspect of this newness which baptism symbolizes: ambitions, motives, and purposes should be new. No longer should life be lived for self but for others and supremely for God. The ultimate question should be not what you and I want but what God wills.

Whose Slave Are You?
(Rom. 6:20,22)

When you were slaves of sin, you were free in regard to righteousness. . . . But now that you have been set free from sin and have become slaves of [to, NIV] God, the return you get is sanctification [holiness, NIV] and its end, eternal life (Rom. 6:20,22).

Some may protest that they are not slaves to anyone or anything. But when properly understood, it becomes quite clear that all of us are in some way and to some degree slaves.

The slavery that Paul referred to here and elsewhere in his epistles was moral and spiritual rather than physical. This means, among other things, that there can be degrees of enslavement.

Many people who loudly proclaim their freedom are really slaves of bad habits and/or a critical, self-defeating spirit or attitude. They may even be slaves of what they consider their freedom.

It is assumed that you, as I, do not claim to be entirely free from the enslavement of sin. Also, we may hesitate to refer to ourselves as slaves of God or Christ as Paul did (Rom. 1:1; Phil. 1:1; Titus 1:1, marginal reading).

We can correctly say, however, that to the degree that we have become slaves of Christ, to that degree we have been made free from the enslavement of sin. Furthermore, we believe that the more we become slaves of Christ, the fuller and richer life will be for us.

The Glorious Promise
(Rom. 8:28)

We know that in everything God works for good with those who love him, who are called according to his purpose (Rom. 8:28).

There are some marvelous promises in the Bible. This is one of the greatest.

This promise, however, has at times been quoted too glibly. All things do not automatically work together for good. No, as the Revised Standard Version says, "God works for good." It is His presence and His presence alone that can make everything work together for good. Notice also it is "with those who love him." It requires their cooperation.

What is His purpose? Paul suggested at least one great overall purpose. The one predominant purpose is that we might be "conformed to the image of his Son" (v. 29). This, our Father is seeking to do, not only through the things that His children suffer but also through all of the experiences of life.

It seems at times that He works in a particular way in the lives of those who suffer, those who carry unusually heavy burdens. Have you noticed that many of your Christian friends who seem to reveal most clearly the image of Christ are those who walk in dark shadows? They have discovered that they have had to walk with the Lord. An awareness of His presence has deepened their lives. Also, as they walk with Him, they have tended to become more conformed to Him and His image.

A "Therefore" of Obligation
(Rom. 12:1)

I appeal to you therefore, brethren, by the mercies of God, to present your bodies as a living sacrifice, holy and acceptable to God, which is your spiritual worship (Rom. 12:1).

"Therefore" in the Old Testament, particularly in the prophets, is usually a "therefore" of judgment. In the New Testament it is usually a "therefore" of responsibility or obligation.

Paul, in the more strictly theological of his epistles, frequently used "therefore" to mark the division between the more theological and the more practical aspects of his epistles (Rom. 12:1; Gal. 5:1; Eph. 4:1). What follows the "therefore" is based primarily on what preceded it.

The "therefore" of Romans 12:1 seems to refer back to all that Paul had said in the first eleven chapters: that all people, Jew and Gentile, were under condemnation for sin; that salvation was available to all through faith in Christ; and that the new life one has through faith in Christ will bring rich blessings into one's life, such as freedom from the law and its condemnation, from the penalty of sin, and freedom to be in the family of God with all of its blessings.

The succeeding exhortations by Paul in Romans will be more meaningful if we use the introductory words in verse 1 as an introduction to each exhortation. For example: "I appeal to you therefore, brethren, by the mercies of God, . . . Do not be not conformed to this world but be transformed."

"Workers for God"
(1 Cor. 3:9)

For we are God's fellow workers (1 Cor. 3:9).

All of us as children of God are "God's fellow workers." We are "partners working together for God" (GNB) in the church and in the kingdom of God. Each one of us should be busy about the work of the Lord. There is a task for every child of God.

His work cannot be done as it should be without the cooperation of all of His children. This is true in the church and in the kingdom in general. No one of us can do all that needs to be done. We need the cooperation of others.

After all, the church is the "body" of Christ, and "just as the body is one and has many members . . . so it is with Christ" (1 Cor. 12:12). The parts of the body must work together in bringing people to Christ, in building the church, and extending the rule and reign of God in the world.

But we must never forget that we are workers for and with God. He is the one who gives the increase. However, He cannot and will not do what He would like to do in our lives, in the church, and in the world without our cooperation.

Also, our work and the work of those who labor with us will be ineffective and unfruitful unless He works with and through us.

Are we seeking as best we can to be workers for God, instruments of His in building His cause in the world?

"The Temple of the Holy Spirit"
(1 Cor. 6:19-20)

Don't you know that your body is the temple [a shrine, NEB] of the Holy Spirit, who lives in you, and who was given to you by God? You do not belong to yourselves but to God; he bought you for a price. So use your bodies for God's glory (1 Cor. 6:19-20, GNB).

Paul, in preceding verses, had suggested that "The body is . . . for the Lord" (v. 13) and that the bodies of Christians "are members of Christ" (v. 15). In the closing verses of this chapter, Paul asked a pointed question: "Don't you know that your body is the temple of the Holy Spirit, who lives in you, the spirit given you by God?"

The Temple stood in the midst of the children of Israel as a symbol of God's presence among them. Christians should be so dedicated to the purposes of God that their bodies will become a temple for the indwelling Spirit. As they walk among people they should be recognized as symbols of the presence of the living God.

Notice also that Paul spelled out the basis for a sense of Christian stewardship for one's body. We do not belong to ourselves but to God.

What is the basis for this ownership? We "have been bought and actually paid for" (Williams). The price was the death of Christ on the cross. What a price! We belong to Him.

Will you not agree that what Paul said in Corinthians about the body should settle many questions that Christians have about what they should or should not do about many of the decisions they have to make every day?

Marriage "in the Lord"
(1 Cor. 7:39)

A wife is bound to her husband as long as he lives. If the husband dies, she is free to be married to whom she wishes, only in the Lord (1 Cor. 7:39).

What did Paul mean by the four words at the close of this statement: "only in the Lord"? Did he mean that the marriage was to be within the will of the Lord? Certainly this should be true of every marriage. But did Paul mean that the one the widow married should be a Christian? The translations of the verse vary, but most of them imply the latter. For example: "Provided the marriage is within the Lord's fellowship" (NEB). Williams plainly says, "Only he must be a Christian." This seems to be what Paul meant.

If Paul would say that a Christian widow should not marry one who was not a Christian, would he not say the same thing concerning those who have never been married? There cannot be a Christian home without a Christian husband and a Christian wife. And we might add that it cannot be a *real* Christian home without a *real* Christian husband and a *real* Christian wife.

In other words, young people, in seeking a life companion, should not only seek one who is a church member but one who is an active, dynamic Christian. This in turn means that the final test will be positive: How much does the spirit of the resurrected Christ find expression in and through his or her life?

Use Liberty Responsibly
(1 Cor. 8:9)

Only take care lest this liberty of yours somehow become a stumbling block to the weak (1 Cor. 8:9).

This basic principle evolved from a problem faced by some of the early Christians. It is discussed to varying degrees in chapters 8, 9, and 10 of 1 Corinthians and in Romans 14.

It seems that meat which was left over from an offering to an idol was sold in the marketplace. Some Christians avoided eating such meat, believing that it would identify them with the worship of the idol.

In contrast, some more "mature" Christians considered it perfectly all right to eat the meat. Paul warned such Christians that their more mature perspective should not be an occasion for the stumbling of a weaker brother.

There are at least two or three more or less basic principles set forth by Paul in his discussion of this problem. Those principles are applicable today. Many Christians through the centuries have found them to be helpful in making decisions concerning right or wrong.

Paul said that if and when we sin against a weaker brother and hurt his conscience, we really sin against Christ (v. 12).

He also said, "Let no one seek his own good, but the good of his neighbor" (1 Cor. 10:24). Another inclusive principle is: "So, whether you eat or drink, or whatever you do, do all to the glory of God (10:31). He then exhorted the Corinthians, and he would exhort us: "Be imitators of me, as I am of Christ."

"The Most Excellent Way"
(1 Cor. 12:31)

I will show you a still more excellent way (1 Cor. 12:31).

Chapter 12 contains Paul's great statement regarding spiritual gifts. The closing sentence of the chapter is, "I will show you the best way of all" (NEB).

There follows a description of love or *agape* as the "most excellent way." How is love the "more excellent" or "best way of all"?

Paul said that it is superior to all other gifts of the Spirit. He mentioned tongues first, which was possibly most highly prized by the Corinthians. Also, note that he used the pronoun *I*. The proper use of pronouns can reveal a great deal about one's attitude toward oneself and toward others.

Then in verses 4 through 7, he described the nature of love with qualities that cannot be duplicated by any other gift or grace.

Also, he suggested that love is the most excellent way because it is superior in its capacity to last. It is contrasted with prophecy, speaking in tongues, and knowledge.

He concluded by saying that faith and hope as well as love abide, but the greatest of these is love. No wonder he said to the Corinthians and would say to us, "Make love [*agape*] your aim" (14:1).

How much do we have of this greatest of all gifts?

An Eschatological "Therefore"
(1 Cor. 15:58)

Therefore, my beloved brethren, be steadfast, immovable, always abounding in the work of the Lord, knowing that in the Lord your labor is not in vain (1 Cor. 15:58).

The "therefore" of judgment is particularly prevalent in the prophets. The "therefore" of obligation or stewardship is especially prominent in the Pauline Epistles (see treasure No. 103 on Rom. 12:1). There is still another type of "therefore": an eschatological "therefore" which involves an exhortation based on hope and assurance.

1 Corinthians 15 is Paul's great chapter on the resurrection. He discussed the resurrection of Christ and the resurrection of the one who is in Christ. At the close of the chapter in a triumphal cry or shout, he said:

"Death is swallowed up in victory."
"O death, where is thy victory?
O death, where is thy sting?"
The sting of death is sin, and the power of sin is the law. But thanks be to God, who gives us the victory through our Lord Jesus Christ (1 Cor. 15:55-57).

It may seem that verse 58 is a strange way to close the mighty resurrection chapter. Paul, however, saw the basis for a practical or moral exhortation in almost every great doctrine or truth.

Here he exhorted the Corinthians, and would exhort us, to be "steadfast, immovable, always abounding in the work of the Lord." What was the basis for Paul's exhortation? It was grounded in what he had said about the resurrection. He himself summed up the reason for his exhortation as follows: "knowing that in the Lord your labor is not in vain [cannot be lost, NEB]."

Divine-Human Nature of the Church
(2 Cor. 1:1; 1 Cor. 1:2)

To the church of God which is at Corinth (2 Cor. 1:1; see 1 Cor. 1:2).

These words suggest that the church is a divine-human institution: "the church of God," its divine nature; "which is at Corinth," its human nature.

A church at Corinth or anywhere else cannot escape its location and the impact of that location on it. A church is also human in the people it reaches and serves. They are very real men and women with distinctive peculiarities, limitations, problems, and sins. To minister to them effectively the church must speak to their needs.

But the church in the contemporary period, as well as in New Testament days, is also a divine institution. It receives its mission or commission and its message from God.

We may be members of a church in the open country, in a village, in a suburb, or of the First Church of Atlanta, Birmingham, Chicago, Dallas, or some other huge metropolitan center. Let us never forget, however, that it is "the church of God." Our churches cannot keep from being influenced by the culture in which they find themselves, but being churches of God they must not be dominated by the culture or become defenders of the culture. As God's churches, they are to deliver God's message *to* the culture.

Let us apply the challenge that comes to churches because of their divine-human nature in one particular area. How can any church claim to be the church of God if it closes its doors to any person because of his or her color, culture, or condition of life?

Stewards of God's Comfort
(2 Cor. 1:3-4)

God of all comfort, who comforts us in all our affliction, so that we may be able to comfort those who are in any affliction [troubles, NEB], with the comfort with which we ourselves are comforted (2 Cor. 1:3-4).

Christians are stewards of every blessing they receive from the Lord. For many of us, one of His greatest blessings is the comfort or help (GNB) that comes from Him. We may have some question concerning some aspects of our faith. There is one thing, however, that many of us can never doubt: the strength and comfort that comes from God will never fail us if we will appropriate it.

There have been times when our family could not have gone on if it had not been for the marvelous comfort which is a gift of God's grace. Our Heavenly Father, as Paul said, is "the Father of mercies and God of *all* comfort" (author's italics). Whatever the occasion, He will supply the strength and comfort that are needed. All we have to do is to accept what He has to offer.

Like other blessings that come into our lives from the Lord, the comfort we have in Him is to be shared with others. Just as we are channels for His love, we are also channels for His comfort, which is an expression of His love. We will be able to pass on to others the comfort that has come to us from Him to the degree to which we have appropriated it for our own lives. The more that comfort has been filtered through our lives and has become a meaningful experience in us and to us, the more meaningful it will be to those with whom we seek to share it.

Let me repeat: we are stewards of the comfort that comes from God, and it is required of stewards that they be found trustworthy or faithful (1 Cor. 4:2).

"A Letter from Christ"
(2 Cor. 3:3)

You are a letter from Christ delivered by us [the result of our ministry, NIV], written not with ink but with the Spirit of the living God, not on tablets of stone but on tablets of human hearts (2 Cor. 3:3).

Paul had just asked the Corinthians, "Do we need, as some do, letters of recommendation to you, or from you?" (v. 1). Then he said, "You yourselves are our letter of recommendation, written on your hearts, to be known and read by all men."

Paul is generally credited with thirteen epistles of the New Testament. But Paul's most effective writing was what he wrote on human hearts and minds that changed the direction of the lives of many people and even of civilization itself.

People of his day and of our day may ignore or grossly misinterpret what Paul wrote in his letters, but they could not and cannot escape the impact of the lives that the Lord through Paul touched and changed. His writings continue to be used by the Lord to touch and change many in our day.

Christians today are "letter[s] from Christ" known and read by all. The pointed question is: What kind of a letter are we? If we claim to be children of God, we can be sure that members of our family, friends, neighbors, and casual acquaintances are reading our lives. For many of them, we will be the only Christian message they will ever read.

What kind of letter are we? Is the message that we deliver crystal clear, or is it poorly structured and difficult to read and understand?

Abundant Harvest
(2 Cor. 9:6)

He who sows sparingly will also reap sparingly, and he who sows bountifully will also reap bountifully (2 Cor. 9:6).

This verse is in the midst of Paul's encouragement for the Corinthians to give to the needy saints at Jerusalem. This offering was a major concern of his.

However, Paul stated in this verse a general principle. It not only relates to the offering for the saints but to giving in general. Furthermore, the principle not only applies to the giving of money and material things but to all of life and life itself.

One who sows "bountifully" or "generously" (NIV) of one's love, concern, and compassion will reap bountifully or generously. The love and appreciation of those who have been loved and touched by that person will be returned. This return or reward will be more highly valued than any possible material reward.

Then there is the inner reward that comes to those who give themselves unselfishly and largely unconsciously in service to others. In other words, they will reap a bountiful inner reward: peace and a deep consciousness of the presence and approval of the divine Spirit.

Furthermore, at the end of the journey we may hear the "well done" of our Heavenly Father. That will be the greatest reward that a child of God can ever receive.

God's Indescribable Gift
(2 Cor. 9:15)

Thanks be to God for his indescribable gift (2 Cor. 9:15, NIV)!

The context of a verse frequently gives it added meaning and significance.

Paul had been discussing, in chapters 8 and 9, the offering for the saints at Jerusalem. It seems that all of a sudden he broke out with a special inspiration: "Thanks be to God for his indescribable (inexpressible, RSV; priceless, GNB) gift beyond words" (NEB)."

There are two possible interpretations of what is meant of "the gift": the grace of God that had led the Gentiles to to share with the saints at Jerusalem or another and more preferable interpretation: the grace of God as expressed in the gift of His Son.

This gift for Paul and also for us was and is indescribable, inexpressible, beyond words.

In what ways is God's gift of Christ inexpressible or indescribable? He was an indescribable Person: He was both God and man.

No one else has ever lived as He lived, loved as He loved, reached out as He did in concern and compassion for people.

This unspeakable gift will provide in our lives, if we permit it to do so, an indescribable presence that will give us a peace that passes all understanding and that will be beyond words to describe.

Have we appropriated all the blessings that can be ours through God's indescribable gift that is available to us?

What Measuring Stick?
(2 Cor. 10:12)

What fools they are to measure themselves by themselves, to find in themselves their own standard of comparison (2 Cor. 10:12, NEB)!

Paul said that those who so measured themselves commended themselves. They could do so because as Christians they were using the wrong measuring stick. Will you not agree that this is a very common fault of many of us as Christians? We tend to measure our lives by the lives of others or we make up our own standards.

But God does not judge us by our standards or by how we may compare to others. He judges us by His expectations of each one of us as individual Christians. It may be that His expectations of you and me are quite different from another member of our family or of our church. He has a unique measurement for each of us and we will be judged by Him on the basis of how we have measured up to His standard.

The supreme overall standard for the Christian is the life of Christ. We have been brought into a vital life-changing union with the resurrected Christ. The test of our lives is how fully we let Him live in us and express Himself through us. In other words, how fully does He possess us? How completely do we walk in the way He walked? Here is a standard for measuring life that will continue to be challenging to us regardless of how mature we may become in the faith.

Life is not to be measured by the lives of others or by standards that we, from the human perspective, have erected in and for our lives. No, the standard is His standard which is perfection.

The Christian Magna Carta
(Gal. 3:28)

There is neither Jew nor Greek, there is neither slave nor free, there is neither male nor female; for you are all one in Christ Jesus (Gal. 3:28).

Williams' translation of the verse is as follows: "There is no room for Jew or Greek, no room for slave or freeman, no room for male or female, for you are all one through union with Christ."

This verse could be called "the human Magna Carta."

Here are listed the major human divisions of Paul's day: Jew and Greek, free and slave, male and female. All could come to Christ in the same way: "In Christ Jesus" they and we "are all sons of God, through faith" (v. 26). That way of faith is open to people regardless of class, color, or condition of life.

This word of Paul is needed by many Christians and churches. After almost two thousand years of teaching and preaching of the Good News of freedom and equality in Christ, many of us and many of our churches are far short of practicing it.

The oneness that Paul proclaimed and that we should proclaim and practice was and is through union with Christ.

We may differ in color of skin, culture, and economic status but if we are children of God we are brothers and sisters in Christ. And if our churches are churches of Christ, they will not turn aside anyone simply because of his color or culture.

Proper Use of Freedom
(Gal. 5:13)

For you were called to freedom, brethren, only do not use your freedom as an opportunity for the flesh, but through love be servants of one another (Gal. 5:13).

Freedom in Christ was a major concern of Paul's. He gave special attention to it in the Galatian letter. In this letter he faced up more specifically than elsewhere the challenge of those who claimed that the Gentile converts had to be circumcised.

For example, he said elsewhere in this chapter, "For freedom Christ has set us free; stand fast therefore, and do not submit again to a yoke of slavery" (Gal. 5:1). Verses 2-12 clearly indicate that "yoke of slavery" referred to circumcision.

It does seem, however, that some of the recent converts in Galatia as well as elsewhere had tended to abuse the new freedom they had discovered in Christ. That freedom needed to be balanced with a sense of responsibility for its proper use.

Christians of every age should be grateful to God for the freedom they have in Christ. Also, they should be aware of the responsibility they have to use that freedom in God-approved ways.

Freedom will be kept in proper control if it is balanced in our lives by a love for others that will express itself in helpful service. The freedom we have as children of God is not a freedom *from* service but a freedom *for* service.

How free are we? What are we doing with our freedom?

"The Fruit of the Spirit"
(Gal. 5:22-23)

But the fruit (harvest, NEB) of the Spirit is love, joy, peace, patience, kindness, goodness, faithfulness, gentleness, self-control (Gal. 5:22-23).

Notice that "love" (*agape*) is the first fruit mentioned. It is basic. The others, to a considerable degree, evolve from it. Love flows into and expresses itself through the others.

Someone has suggested that there are three clusters of the fruit: (1) inner qualities—love, joy, peace; (2) qualities that express themselves in relations with others—patience, kindness, goodness; (3) general character traits—faithfulness or fidelity (NEB), gentleness or humility (TEV), and temperance or self-control.

We should remember that fruit is natural. The nature of the fruit depends on the nature of the tree. A peach tree bears peaches; an apple tree bears apples. It is just as natural, even as inevitable, that a Christian will bear some fruit of the Spirit as it is that a peach tree will bear peaches.

The amount of fruit may vary from life to life and from season to season. But we have no basis on which to be called "children of God" unless there is some evidence of the fruit of the Spirit in our lives.

There are few passages of Scripture that will search our souls any more than this one if we will let it. Using letter grades (A,B,C,D,F), how would you grade yourself on each fruit mentioned? Would you make a passing grade on each one? What about the nine as a whole?

Branded for Jesus
(Gal. 6:17)

From now on let no one cause trouble for me, for I bear on my body the brand-marks of Jesus (Gal. 6:17, NASB).

The Good News Bible says, "The scars I have on my body show that I am the slave of Jesus."

West Texas State University has a collection of famous branding irons. Branding was an important aspect of ranching in the West in the days of the open range. The brand on cattle or on horses was proof of ownership at the time of the roundup.

Branding was important in other ways in biblical times. Captives and slaves were frequently branded with the name of their owner. Those who have been captured by or are slaves of Christ should have his mark branded or stamped on them.

For Paul those brands or marks of ownership by the Lord were his scars. Our brands are not physical brands or marks. Whatever brands or marks we have for Christ are inner and spiritual in the main. It is true that our baptism is an outer symbol of ownership. It is meaningless, however, unless there are some deeper and more significant brands or marks within our own souls.

That which is inner, however, cannot help but manifest itself outwardly. Can those about us in the home, on the street, where we work and play see some marks of Jesus in our lives? Have we really been branded by Him and for Him?

Faith and Works
(Eph. 2:8-10)

For by grace you have been saved through faith; and this is not your own doing, it is the gift of God—not because of works, lest any man should boast. For we are his workmanship, created in Christ Jesus for good works, which God prepared beforehand, that we should walk in them (Eph. 2:8-10).

There has been and is considerable discussion of the relation of faith and works in the Christian's life. An examination of Paul's writings will reveal that he had a balanced emphasis. No one passage in his epistles reveals this more clearly than these three verses in Ephesians. There are at least two important truths concerning faith and works that are stated in these verses.

First, Paul plainly said here as elsewhere that salvation is a product of God's grace apart from works. Through faith persons can appropriate that salvation.

There is a second great truth in these verses. It is frequently neglected. That truth is that we are "created in Christ Jesus for good works" or "to devote ourselves to the good deeds for which God has designed us" (NEB).

The preceding is so true that good deeds or good works are proof that we have been saved. James said, "Prove to me that this faith you speak of is real though not accompanied by deeds, and by my deeds I will prove to you my faith" (Jas. 2:18, NEB). Jesus plainly said, "You will know them by their fruits" (Matt. 7:16, 20).

Faith and works belong together. One is cause, the other, effect. How closely are they related in our lives? How much outer evidence is there of an inner faith that has brought salvation to us through our union with the resurrected Christ.

A Worthy Walk
(Eph. 4:1)

I, therefore, the prisoner for the Lord, beg you to lead a life worthy of the calling to which you have been called (Eph. 4:1).

The Good News Bible translates the latter part of this verse as follows: "Live a life that measures up to the standard God set when he called you." What was and is that standard? Will you not agree that the standard is for us to be like the One with whom we have been brought into union?

What is the calling to which Paul referred? It seems relatively clear that it meant the original call to be a Christian.

Paul mentioned in verse 2 some qualities that characterize the worthy walk: lowliness or humility, gentleness or meekness, forbearance or patience.

The word *walk* is found three times in the fifth chapter of Ephesians. Each of these might properly be considered an evidence or an expression of a walk that is worthy of our calling as Christians. The Ephesians were admonished to "walk in love" (5:2), to "walk as children of light" (5:8), and to "walk circumspectly" (5:15, KJV) or to "Look carefully" how they walked.

This is the high or upward call of God. Surely we will admit that we have not yet attained or expressed fully that high calling. Can we say with Paul, "I press on toward the goal for the prize of the upward call of God in Christ Jesus" (Phil. 3:14).

A Misplaced Comma
(Eph. 4:11-12)

His gifts were that some should be apostles, some prophets, some evangelists, some pastors and teachers, to equip the saints for the work of ministry, for building up the body of Christ (Eph. 4:11-12).

The placing of a comma can make a great deal of difference in the meaning of a sentence. The comma after "saints" in the King James Version's translation of the Scripture quoted above does not belong there. With the comma there, "the perfecting of the saints" (KJV) and so forth are the purpose or responsibility of the apostles, prophets, evangelists, pastors and teachers.

The Good News Bible translates this passage as follows: "It was he who 'gave gifts to mankind'; he appointed some to be apostles, others to be prophets, others to be evangelists, others to be pastors and teachers. He did this to prepare all God's people for the work of

Christian service, in order to build up the body of Christ." In other words, the primary task of the uniquely called ones is "to equip the saints" that they may do "the work of ministry" and so forth.

The comma needs to be removed, not only in the translation of the Scripture, but also in its application ta the work of our churches. The work of the churches should be done in the main by the laypersons of the churches. The chief responsibility of the staff, whether one or many, should be to train the lay members to perform their task more effectively. It is true, however, that demonstration is a most important aspect of teaching and training.

The Measure of a Man
(Eph. 4:13)

Until we all attain . . . to mature manhood, to the measure of the stature of the fulness of Christ (Eph. 4:13).

This Scripture is in that marvelous passage about the work of the prophets, evangelists, pastors, teachers cited in the previous treasure. Paul said that their task was to equip the saints and that the latter, along with the former, were to do the work of ministry. An important phase of that work was and is that the saints as Christians might attain a "perfect measure of Christ's moral stature" (Williams).

The more we move in that direction, the clearer we will see that we are far from attaining that stature. We do not expect to measure up fully even when we reach the end of life's journey. We do believe, however, that this is a standard by which Christians should measure their lives. No other standard is adequate; and none other will continue to challenge us as we mature in and for Christ.

How tall do we stand when measured by Christ's moral stature? How tall in the home, the church, or the community? This is possibly even more important: Are we taller today than yesterday, this week than last week, this month than last month, this year than last year?

The supreme question is not: Are we mature? but: Are we moving toward "mature manhood, measured by nothing less than the full stature of Christ" (NEB)? The answer we can give to this question depends on the vitality of our relationship to the One who is not only

the measure of our maturity but also the means by which we mature
or grow.

"Husbands, Love Your Wives"
(Eph. 5:25)

Husbands, love your wives, as Christ loved the church and gave himself
up for her (Eph. 5:25).

Paul, in this beautiful passage (Eph. 5:22-33), compared the relation of husband and wife to the relation of Christ and His church. He
suggested that just as the church is subject to Christ, so the wife
should be submissive to her husband.

In turn, Paul said that husbands should love their wives as their
own bodies (v. 28) or as they love themselves (v. 33), which is possibly
simply another way of saying the same thing. His highest admonition
is that the husband love his wife as Christ loved the church (v. 25).
How much did Christ love the church? He loved it enough that He
gave His life for it.

The word for *love* here is the distinctly New Testament word *agape*.
In other words, the husband is to love his wife with the same quality
of love with which Christ loved the church and with which God loved
the world (John 3:16).

Wives may chafe at Paul's admonition for them to submit to their
husbands. Will you not agree, however, that very few wives would
object to submitting themselves to their husbands if their husbands
loved them as Christ loved the church?

And it is doubtful if a wife is any more obligated to be submissive
to her husband than he is obligated to love her as Christ loved the
church.

"The Upward Call of God"
(Phil. 3:14)

I press on toward the goal for the prize of the upward call of God in
Christ Jesus (Phil. 3:14).

This verse needs to be read in its context. For example, Paul said in verse 10, "That I may know him and the power of his resurrection." In verses 12 and 13 Paul said, "Not that I have already obtained this or am already perfect; but I press on to make it my own, . . . I do not consider that I have made it my own." Then notice what he said, "But one thing I do, forgetting what lies behind and straining forward to what lies ahead, I press on toward the goal for the prize of the upward call of God in Christ Jesus."

Paul was evidently a close observer of the athletic games of that day. Some of his terms in this statement are drawn from the races: "press on," "forgetting what lies behind," and "straining forward."

The goal of a race was frequently a piece of statuary. The winner was the one who could first complete the race and touch that statue. Jesus is the goal of the Christian's race. Paul, here as elsewhere, did not claim that he had won the race or attained the goal of his race.

If he was conscious of falling short of "the upward call of God in Christ Jesus," how much more should that be true of you and me? As we move closer to the goal (likeness to Christ), we become increasingly conscious of the fact that the goal moves forward but never out of sight. Can we say with Paul, "I press on." Do we feel the tug to come on higher?

Strength for the Task
(Phil. 4:13)

I can do all things in him who strengthens me (Phil. 4:13).

The general background for this statement by Paul was the concern of the Philippians for his physical needs. They had shared in his support as he went elsewhere with the gospel (4:15-16).

The immediate background is: "I have learned the secret of facing plenty and hunger, abundance and want" (v. 12). Paul said that regardless of external circumstances he could do all things in Him (Christ) who strengthened him.

It was the indwelling Christ that enabled Paul to say, "I know how to be abased, and I know how to abound" (v. 12). Paul had learned or acquired the secret of accepting life as it came. He had the marvelous capacity that many of us need to acquire: the habit of resting in the Lord.

Paul had the same general attitude toward the tasks that he faced for the Lord. Whatever God wanted him to do, he had confidence that the Father would provide the guidance and strength he needed.

When asked to teach a class, lead a group, serve as a deacon or chairman of a committee, or do something in the church, do we say, "I can't?"? The main question should be: "Does the Father want me to do it? If He does, then He will give me the strength that is needed."

The same is true for any task or call of God, including the call to vocational religious service. If it is His call, we should respond, knowing that He will give the strength that will be needed.

What a Prayer!
(Col. 1:9)

So, from the day we heard of it, we have not ceased to pray for you (Col. 1:9).

We do not know much about Paul's prayer life. We do know that he prayed for the churches he had founded and visited. For example, he prayed for those at Rome (Rom. 1:9), the Ephesians (Eph. 1:16), the Philippians (Phil. 1:4), and the Thessalonians (2 Thess. 1:11), as well as the Colossians.

Paul wrote the Colossians that he had not ceased to pray for them. In other words, he had not simply breathed a prayer when Epaphras told him of the Colossians' love for him. Paul's response was not so much to thank them or to express his gratitude to God for them. He obviously did that, but his main response was to pray for them.

Notice some of the things he prayed for: that they might be "filled with the knowledge of his [God's] will . . . to lead a life [walk in a manner, NASB] worthy of the Lord, fully pleasing to him, bearing fruit in every good work and increasing [grow, NEB] in the knowledge of God" (vv. 9-10).

He also prayed that they might be "strengthened with all power, according to his glorious might, for all endurance [steadfastness, NASB; fortitude, NEB] and patience with joy, giving thanks to the

Father, who has qualified us to share in the inheritance of the saints in light" (vv. 11-12).

How comprehensive and consistent are our prayer lives?

Another "Therefore" of Obligation
(Col. 2:6)

As therefore you received Christ Jesus the Lord, so live in him (Col. 2:6).

As suggested in a former treasure the word *therefore* is an important word in both Testaments. In the Old Testament it is usually a "therefore" of judgment. The children of Israel had sinned; "therefore," the judgment of God was coming to them. In the New Testament, especially in Paul's epistles, it is usually a "therefore" of obligation or responsibility. The basis for the obligation was what God had done. Outstanding examples referred to earlier are Romans 12:1 and Ephesians 4:1.

Here in Colossians, Paul was speaking to them, and would speak to us, as individuals. As children of God they and we have "received Christ Jesus the Lord." We are in Him, and He is in us.

This experience is not exclusively a blessing to be received. Certainly, we should be deeply grateful for the life we have in Him, but this experience that made us new creations in Christ Jesus places some responsibility on us as it did on the Colossians.

We are under obligation to live our "lives in union with him" (NEB). As best we can, we should let Him live in us and express Himself through us. We will never do this fully or perfectly.

Do we recognize, however, that this is an essential phase of the Christian life? Furthermore, are we making progress living as we should live, or, possibly better, are we increasingly letting Him live in us and express Himself more fully through us?

The Resurrected Life
(Col. 3:1)

Since, then, you have been raised with Christ (Col. 3:1, NIV).

The first word in most versions is *if.* The *if,* however, is not an *if* of conjecture but of assumption.

When were the Colossians raised with Christ? Ideally, when He arose from the grave. Actually or biographically, when they came into union with Him at the time of their conversion. So it is with us.

Paul proceeded to describe the kind of life the Colossians should live since they had been raised with Christ. There are at least three distinct aspects of that life.

First, he exhorted them to "Practice occupying your minds with the things above" (v. 2, Williams). The Colossians had been raised with Christ; they should seek the things where He is.

Also, they should "once for all" put to death their earthly nature (v. 5). He spelled out specifically some of the sins and vices that are out of harmony with living the resurrected life.

Then, as is typical in the Bible, the negative is balanced and climaxed by a statement of the positive aspects of the resurrected life. What a challenge in the virtues listed!

He closed with the exhortation: "And above (over, Williams) all these things put on love, which binds everything together in perfect harmony" (v. 14).

There is enough in what Paul said concerning the resurrected life to challenge us for the rest of life's journey. How do we measure up?

"More and More"
(1 Thess. 4:1)

Finally, brethren, we beseech [request, NASB] and exhort you in the Lord Jesus, that . . . you ought to live and to please God, just as you are doing, you do so more and more (1 Thess. 4:1).

The words *more and more* appear one other place in this chapter in 1 Thessalonians. Paul reminded them that they had been taught by God to love one another. He commended them, saying that they did love the brethren of Macedonia. He then added, "But we exhort you, brethren, to do so more and more" (4:10).

Earlier, in the same epistle, he had said, "May the Lord make you increase and abound in love to one another and to all men, as we do to you" (3:12). This is the "more and more" perspective without the use of those words, a perspective that is very prevalent in Paul's epistles.

He said of himself, "Not that I have already obtained this or am already perfect; but I press on to make my own, because Christ Jesus has made me his own" (Phil. 3:12; see treasure No. 125).

If that was true of Paul, how much more true it is of you and me. But are we, like him, pressing on "toward the goal for the prize of the upward call of God in Christ Jesus" (Phil. 3:14)?

Do we feel the tug of the upward call of God, the challenge of "more and more": more love, more compassion and concern, more living like He would have us live in the home, the church, the community, and the world?

Worthy of God's Call
(2 Thess. 1:11)

To this end we always pray for you, that our God may make you worthy of his call, and may fulfill every good resolve and work of faith by his power (2 Thess. 1:11).

Paul exhorted the Ephesians to live a life worthy of the calling to which they had been called (Eph. 4:1; see treasure 121). He told the Thessalonians that he prayed for them that God would make them worthy of His call.

There is no conflict between the exhortation to the Ephesians to walk worthy and the prayer of Paul that God would enable the Thessalonians to walk worthy. Their efforts and God's help were both necessary.

We should do what we can to live a life worthy of the calling of God, but we cannot fully live that kind of life without our Father's help. We can be just as sure that He will help us if we will do what we can to help ourselves. God will always meet us more than halfway if we make an honest attempt to walk in His way and hence in a way worthy of His calling.

Even if "call" refers to some experience subsequent to the original call to be a Christian, Paul would still remind us that we should seek to walk worthy of that call or calling. Also, he would say that we will need the help of the Lord if we are to be worthy of God's call. It is doubtful if any of us are ever fully worthy of the call of God to serve Him and our fellow human beings.

Empty-Handed
(1 Tim. 6:7)

We brought nothing into the world, and we cannot take anything out of the world (1 Tim. 6:7).

Spiritual treasures are the only ones that we can take with us into the next world. Why should so many of us give so much of our energy, time, and thought to the accumulation of money and material things?

Later in this same chapter, Paul said that the "love of money is the root of all evils [all kinds of evil, NIV]; it is through this craving that some have wandered away from the faith and pierced their hearts with many pangs" (v. 10). We should not forget, however, that the love of money and material things is not exclusively the sin of the rich. We may have little of this world's goods and yet be lovers of money and the things it can buy.

One of the richest men in our city had died. A group of his friends were visiting at the funeral home with members of his family. In the midst of the conversation one asked the question, "I wonder how much he left?" Another friend with a Christian perspective said, "He left all that he had." That closed the conversation.

It is good for all of us who are in the family of God to remember that whether we have little or much, we will have to leave it behind when we go to meet the Father.

We should be possessors of and not be possessed by what we have. Money and things material should never be permitted to enslave us. They may be good servants but should never be our masters.

Christ-Centered Confidence
(2 Tim. 1:12)

And therefore I suffer as I do; But I am not ashamed, for I know whom I have believed [trusted, NEB] and I am sure [convinced, NASB; confident, NEB] that He is able to guard until that Day what has been entrusted to Me (2 Tim. 1:12).

The time when and the conditions under which words are spoken or written frequently give them added significance. Paul had had many years of experiences in and with the resurrected Christ. Also, he wrote from prison. His execution was a possibility at any time (4:6). Even when faced with death because of his ministry for Jesus, Paul said, "I know whom I have believed." His was a Christ-centered confidence.

Paul certainly knew what he believed as well as any Christian who has ever lived. He did not say, however, "I know *what* I believe" but "I know *whom*" (author's italics). Our faith should be and ultimately must be primarily centered in a Person, in Christ.

Paul had many associates and friends, some of whom deserted him when the going was rough. He even said, "No one stood by me the first time I defended myself; all deserted me" (4:16, GNB). But then notice what he said: "But the Lord stood by me and gave me strength" (v. 17). It is no wonder that Paul would say, "I know . . . him."

The more mature we are in Christ, the more we will be able to say with assurance: "I know Him." In turn, the better we know Him, the more complete will be our commitment to Him and to His way and will in our lives.

House Churches
(Philem. 1-2)

Paul . . . To Philemon . . . and Apphia our sister and Archippus our fellow soldier, and the church in your house (Philem. 1-2).

This term "the church in your house" is found three other places in Paul's epistles (1 Cor. 16:19; Rom. 16:5; Col. 4:15). The first two of these references were to churches in the home of that wonderful couple Paul first met in Corinth, Aquilla and Priscilla.

The statement refers to churches meeting in the homes of the people. Even today such "house churches" or missions are frequently found, particularly on mission fields. Many wonderful churches have begun in the homes of Christians.

Will you not agree, however, that these two God-ordained institutions—church and home—are closely related in many ways? The church is or should be a spiritual family. We are brothers and sisters in Christ. We have the same Heavenly Father, and the family spirit should characterize our relations to one another.

Likewise, the Christian home can be and should be a church. Both it and the church have some distinctive functions, but they also have some common functions. Among the functions they share are the evangelistic, teaching, and worship functions.

Also, the more fully the family becomes a church the greater will be its contribution to the work of the church. Likewise, the more the family spirit permeates the church, the greater will be its contribution to families and to the members of those families.

A Christian home can and should be a little church. Is your home and mine performing some of the functions of a church?

Help in Time of Temptation
(Heb. 4:15)

We have not a high priest who is unable to sympathize with our weaknesses, but one who in every respect has been tempted as we are, yet without sin (Heb. 4:15).

The writer previously had said that because Jesus had "suffered and been tempted, he is able to help those who are tempted" (2:18). Here in 4:15 he went a little farther. He said we have a high priest who can sympathize with our weaknesses. Being fully human as well as divine, Jesus had been tempted with the same kind of temptations that we have had.

The fact that "in every respect [He] has been tempted as we are" assures us of a sympathetic, understanding Lord and Savior.

"Yet without sin" is our hope of victory. He did not sin. We can have His help. That is our source of victory.

Because all of this is true, the writer said, "Let us then with confidence draw near to the throne of grace, that we may receive mercy and find grace to help in time of need" (v. 16).

God's grace is expressed in His forgiveness when we have sinned. His grace is also available for victory over the temptations that press on us from every side.

Without any claim that we live or can live entirely free from sin, will you not agree that many of us go around defeated in our lives because we do not seek from our risen Lord the strength that we need for that victory?

The Fairness of God
(Heb. 6:10)

God is not unfair. He will not forget the work you did or the love you showed for him in the help you gave and are still giving to your fellow Christians (Heb. 6:10, GNB).

The God we worship and serve is not an unfair or unjust God. One evidence that He is not unfair is the fact that He will not forget. Three things are suggested in this verse that He will not forget.

(1) He will not forget or overlook the *work* we do. Others may overlook it but not God. Ours may be a big or a little task. Whether big or little, He will not forget or overlook what we do. If faithful we will receive His commendation at the end of the journey and His "well done" should be sufficient reward.

(2) He will not forget or overlook the *love* we show for Him and for our fellow humans in His name. When we joined the resurrected Christ we were brought into union with *agape* or love: "God is [*agape*]" (1 John 4:8,16). His love should reach out through us to all kinds of persons. God will not forget or overlook any expression through us of His love for those about us.

(3) God will not forget or overlook the *help* we give or have given to fellow Christians and, we could add, to any person who is in need. Such help is a product of our love for them. This love is a product of His love for us and for them. He wants to love fellow believers and all people through us.

Let us summarize: God is not unfair or unjust, as evidenced by the fact that He will not forget or overlook the work we do, the love we share, or the help we give. Will we hear His "well done" at the end of the journey?

"Pleasures of Sin"
(Heb. 11:24-25)

By faith Moses, . . . refused to be called the son of Pharaoh's daughter, choosing rather to share ill-treatment with the people of God than to enjoy the fleeting pleasures of sin (Heb. 11:24-25).

These verses are in the great chapter that calls the roll of the faithful: Abel, Enoch, Noah, Abraham, Isaac, Jacob, Joseph, Moses, and others. Moses made a decision that changed the whole direction of his life and brought him into line with the purposes of God.

There are two suggestions concerning sin in these verses from Hebrews. First, sin may be and frequently is enjoyable. This may not be true of all forms of sin, but if some sins did not give pleasure they would not appeal so strongly to many Christians as well as non-Christians.

The second suggestion concerning sin is that the pleasures of sin are "fleeting" or "transient" (NEB). Sooner or later the pleasure is gone.

Sometimes the pleasure derived from sin is short-lived. Many people have thought they had a "great time," but by the time they got alone in their rooms they hated themselves for what they had done. Or, they may awaken the next morning wondering how they could have done what they did the night before.

In contrast, the penalty of sin may linger for a considerable period of time. We can be sure that sooner or later there will be either inner regret or judgment. In some way we pay a price for the sins we commit. What little pleasure there is in sin will be "fleeting." Has this been your experience?

Seeing the Invisible
(Heb. 11:27)

By faith he left Egypt, not being afraid of the anger of the king; for he endured [persevered, NIV] as seeing him who is invisible (Heb. 11:27).

This verse comes from the great roll call of the faithful recorded in Hebrews 11. More space is given to Abraham and Moses than to any of the others.

Notice some things that Moses gave up in response to his vision of the invisible One. He refused to be called "the son of Pharaoh's daughter" (v. 24); "to enjoy the pleasures of sin for a season" (v. 25, KJV)—they are always only "for a season"; and "the treasures of Egypt" (v. 26).

What was the secret to the fact that Moses turned away from things that most men would have held onto? It was because he had seen the invisible One.

What was true of Moses and others mentioned in the roll call has been true through the centuries of many of God's pioneering prophetic spirits. They have been men and women who have seen the invisible One or heard a word from Him. They have been willing to run risks in response to His call and way for them. They go to their God-ordained tasks with a Bible in their hands and a transcendent point of reference in their hearts.

Have we had a glimpse of the Invisible One? What has been, and what is our response to that glimpse? Our response will largely determine the contribution we will make to the cause of Christ and to the world in which we live. It ultimately will determine, to a large degree, the sense of fulfillment we will have in our lives.

Running a Good Race
(Heb. 12:1-2)

Therefore, since we are surrounded by so great a cloud of witnesses, let us also lay aside every weight, and sin which clings so closely, and let us run with perseverance the race that is set before us, looking to Jesus the pioneer and perfecter of our faith (Heb. 12:1-2).

Four things concerning the Christian race are suggested in these verses.

(1) *Incentive for running the race:* "since we are surrounded by so great a cloud of witnesses." These included the roll call of the faithful in the preceding chapter. For us there are many others: Christian martyrs through the centuries, our Christian parents, grandparents, and many others. They are looking down on us as we run our race.

(2) *Preparation for the race:* We should lay aside anything that will hinder or handicap us in running the Christian race. This includes "sin which clings so closely" to us or "every sin to which we cling" (NEB).

(3) *The perseverance or determination (GNB) with which the race is run:* The winner of the race is not always the swiftest. Persistence or determination is as important a factor in running the Christian race as it is for the 440 or the 880.

(4) Notice also "the race that is set before us" or "the race for which we are entered" (NEB). *Each one has his or her own distinctive race to run.*

(5) *The goal of the race:* "looking to Jesus." We are to fix our eyes on Him and measure our lives by Him.

Have we made Him the goal of our Christian race? Are we moving toward that goal?

Doers and Hearers
(Jas. 1:22)

Prove yourselves doers of the word, and not merely hearers who delude themselves (Jas. 1:22, NASB).

James plainly said, "Keep on obeying this message" (Williams) or "put it into practice" (GNB). One who does not do anything about the message one hears deceives or deludes oneself.

One will not know what to put into practice unless one clearly hears the word. The admonition of James, however, is that they do more than just hear the message.

A church in Tulsa, Oklahoma, has something in its sanctuary that symbolizes what James was saying. At the front behind the pulpit is a beautiful stained-glass window with a cross as the central emblem. As the congregation leaves after the worship service there is a prominent figure of a yoke in the window at the rear of the sanctuary.

We go to church to worship the crucified and risen Christ; we go or should go from that worship service yoked together as a Christian body and yoked with Him to minister to others for Him.

William Barclay wrote, "That which is heard in the holy place must be lived in the marketplace or there is no point in hearing it."

Really, some of the most rewarding worship experiences that we may have can be when we are seeking to carry out the instruction and inspiration that came to us when we joined with loved ones and friends in the worship of God.

Social and Personal Morality
(Jas. 1:27)

Religion that is pure and undefiled before God the Father is this: to visit orphans and widows in their affliction [distress, NASB, NIV], and to keep oneself unstained [untarnished, NEB; from being polluted, NIV] from the world (Jas. 1:27).

This verse summarizes what James called pure and undefiled religion. A portion of this verse could have been lifted from the prophets. The God revealed by the prophets and in the Old Testament in general had a special concern for the underprivileged, including widows and orphans. The Epistle of James is generally considered more closely related in its perspective to the Old Testament than any other New Testament book.

There is a balancing in this verse of personal and social morality that is needed. Too frequently one or the other is neglected. Strength in one area is not and cannot be an adequate substitute for the other.

For example, the strictest adherence to high personal moral standards cannot be substituted for a concern and compassion for people and particularly for the neglected and underprivileged. Neither can it substitute for a concern about and active involvement in many of the social and moral issues in our society.

In contrast, a concern about moral and social conditions does not excuse a Christian from maintaining high standards of personal morality. The choice should not be an "either/or" but a "both/and."

In which area is our strength and weakness? What can we do to have a better balance in our lives between the two?

Faith and Works
(Jas. 2:26)

> For as the body apart from the spirit is dead, so faith apart from works is dead (Jas. 2:26); As the body is dead when there is no breath left in it, so faith divorced from deeds is lifeless as a corpse (NEB).

For a complete picture of what James said concerning the relation of faith and works one needs to read verses 14-26 of this chapter.

James started with two questions: "What does it profit . . . if a man says he has faith but has not works? Can his [that, NEB; such, NIV] faith save him?" (v. 14). His answer: "Faith by itself, if has no works, is dead" (v. 17).

James was not saying that one is saved by works. He was stressing, however, that the kind of faith that saves is faith that will produce some good works.

His conclusion is that just as when the spirit leaves the body that person is dead, so in like manner so-called faith apart from works is dead.

While this is possibly the most direct statement of the relation of faith and works in the New Testament, it is not the only place where this relationship is emphasized.

Good deeds or works do not save us, but they are the evidence or proof that we have been saved.

Our salvation which comes through faith is not simply a gift to be enjoyed; it is also an obligation to be fulfilled.

Do our works or our lives demonstrate to others and prove to ourselves that we have been brought into union with the resurrected Christ?

A Holy People
(1 Pet. 2:9)

You are a chosen race, a royal priesthood, a holy nation, God's own people (1 Pet. 2:9).

The Old Testament provides the background for an understanding of this statement by Peter. Israel, from God's perspective, was "a holy [dedicated, NEB] nation, God's own people."

God, who is holy, expects holiness of His people. The basic idea of holiness in the Old Testament was two directional: separation *from* the world and the sins of the world and separation *to* God and His will and purposes.

So it is with the new Israel. We, the contemporary children of God, are to be separated *from* the world and *to* the will and purposes of God. Peter stated one specific purpose of our separation: "that you may declare the wonderful deeds of him who called you out of darkness unto his marvelous light" (v. 9*b*).

This separation is interpreted by some as actual physical separation from the world. Although we do not believe that our Father expects us to withdraw from the world, He does want His people of every age to separate themselves from the sins of the world.

Peter specifically mentioned some things that will characterize a holy or separated people: "Keep on abstaining from the evil desires of your lower nature" (v. 11, Williams) and "Keep on living upright lives among the heathen" (v. 12, Williams).

Are we holy or separated? What about your church home and mine? Do they have the characteristics of a new Israel?

Free Persons: God's Slaves
(1 Pet. 2:16)

Live as free people; do not, however, use your freedom to cover up any evil, but live as God's slaves (1 Pet. 2:16, GNB).

This verse expresses one of many meaningful paradoxes in our biblical faith: we are free but slaves. Some of the other paradoxes are that greatness comes through service, exhaltation through humility, life through death. All of these are made understandable and meaningful by the greatest of the paradoxes: victory comes by way of the cross.

One of the most marvelous paradoxes is the fact that the more completely we become slaves of God, the freer we are. Paul plainly suggests that we are enslaved either to sin and Satan or to Christ and righteousness (see Rom. 6:16,18,20,22). No wonder he so frequently spoke of himself as the bond servant or slave of Christ.

There is another aspect of the freedom we have in Christ. The freedom that is ours in Him is to be voluntarily surrendered for the sake of others. Paul said, "For you were called to freedom, brethren; only do not use your freedom as an opportunity for the flesh, but through love be servants of one another" (Gal. 5:13). Of himself Paul said, "For though I am free from all men, I have made myself a slave to all, that I might win the more" (1 Cor. 9:19).

In other words, we are slaves of Christ and slaves of others for Christ. But let us repeat: it is through enslavement that the Christian discovers real freedom.

A Ladder of Virtues
(2 Pet. 1:5,7)

Make every effort [do your level best, Williams] to supplement your faith with virtue, and virtue with knowledge, . . . and godliness with brotherly affection, and brotherly affection with love (2 Pet. 1:5,7).

Lists of virtues and vices were rather common in New Testament days. They were used by secular as well as biblical writers. Paul has several such lists in his epistles. Possibly the most widely known is his "fruit of the Spirit" (Gal. 5:19-23).

Our main interest in Peter's list is where he began and where he closed. The first rung or step is *faith*. This is the beginning point in the Christian life. All other virtues depend on it and flow from it.

The top rung of Peter's ladder of virtues is *love*. Faith looks to God; love (*agape*) looks out to human beings in the name of God. Notice that love is to be added to brotherly love. Love of the brethren is a wonderful virtue, but our love has not reached the level of God's *agape* until it reaches out to all people.

There can be and should be a special love for those in the Christian family, but Christian love cannot be restricted to the Christian circle. It inevitably will spill over to the larger world community.

Notice what Peter said following the listing of the virtues: "For if these things are yours and abound, they keep you from being ineffective or unfruitful in the knowledge of our Lord Jesus Christ" (v. 8).

How much are these qualities found in our lives? Have we reached the top rung of the ladder (*agape*)?

Grow in Grace
(2 Pet. 3:18)

Grow in the grace and knowledge of our Lord and Savior Jesus Christ (2 Pet. 3:18).

This is the closing admonition of this short epistle.

We are saved by grace. We need to grow ("continue to grow," Williams) in that grace. When we were born into the kingdom of God we were newborn in Christ. Being in Christ, however, assures some growth. The extent and the rate of that growth will depend on how much we let the grace of God that saved us find expression in our lives.

Peter's admonition was not only very relevant for those to whom he wrote, but it is equally appropriate for us today. We need to appropriate the grace of God that is available to us. In other words, we need to comprehend more fully and to utilize more completely the grace of God that will enable us to have the victory over the temptations of life and to express more fully and naturally something of His spirit in our relations to others in every area of our lives. There are entirely too many of us who should be mature Christians who are still sickly and anemic in our Christian growth.

Let each one of us take seriously Peter's admonition that we grow in grace and in our "knowledge of our Lord and Savior Jesus Christ." Knowledge is a product of the grace of God, and in turn that knowledge will give to us a deepened sense of dependence on and a clearer insight into the nature and significance of the grace of God.

Walk in His Way
(1 John 2:5-6)

By this we may be sure that we are in him: he who says he abides in him ought to walk in the same way in which he walked (1 John 2:5-6).

If we are Christians the resurrected Christ lives in us and we in Him. In other words, if we claim to be Christians we are saying that we abide in Him.

John said that we can be sure that we are in Him if we "walk in the same way in which he walked." We may not and will not succeed in walking fully or perfectly in that way. We will acknowledge, however, that we "ought" to walk in the way in which He walked or "live as Christ himself lived" (NEB). That is the norm or standard toward which we strive and by which we should measure our lives.

If we walked in the way He walked or lived as He lived, where would it take us? He was supremely concerned about people. He had compassion on people. He unselfishly ministered to the needs of people. He went about doing good (Acts 10:38). These things will be true of us as we walk in the way in which He walked.

If we walked all the way with Him it would take us into and through the garden, "up Calvary's mountain," and into the tomb, but, thank the Lord, also through or out of the tomb. Resurrection always follows real crucifixion. We have been raised with Him to walk in newness of life—a life given in service to Him and for Him to our fellow human beings.

God's Love
(1 John 3:17)

But if any one has the world's goods and sees his brother in need, yet closes his heart against him, how does God's love abide in him? (1 John 3:17).

Notice that it does not say: "How does the love of his brother abide in him?" but: "How does God's love abide in him?"

There are two major interpretations of these phrases. One is that it refers to the love one has *for* God: "How can he claim that he loves God?" (GNB).

The other view is that it refers to the love that comes from God: "How can it be said that the divine love dwells in him?" (NEB)

The first interpretation stresses the fact that love for our fellow human beings is proof of our love for God.

The second interpretation stresses the fact that God's children are channels for His love for people.

Whichever interpretation is correct, our preference is the second, a relevant and searching question that might and should be asked us: "Will we let the love of God flow through us to reach out and bless the lives of those we touch?" God has always showed an unusual concern for those in need: the widowed, the orphan, the needy, and the underprivileged in general. He would like to use us to reach these for Him.

The love from God that seeks to reach out to others through us is to be practical in its expression. It is not to be a vapory sentiment. John, in the very next verse, said, "My children, our love should not be just words and talk; it must be true love, which shows itself in action" (GNB).

How much of that kind of love do we have?

The Source of Love
(1 John 4:19)

We love, because he first loved us (1 John 4:19).

The King James Version translates this verse as follows: "We love him, because he first loved us." God's love for us calls forth, or at least it should call forth, a corresponding love for Him. But an even more significant truth is the fact that love characterizes or at least should characterize our lives because He first loved us.

When we were brought into union with Him in our initial Christian experience, we were brought into union with love. John elsewhere in this epistle said, "God is love" (1 John 4:8,16).

God's love (*agape*) is a self-giving love. He "so loved the world that he gave his only Son, that whoever believes in him should not perish but have eternal life" (John 3:16).

Since we have been brought into union with love, it is not only natural but inevitable that love will find some expression in our lives. The more vital that relationship, the more certain and extensive will be the outreach of God's love (*agape*) through us to others.

How much does love abide in us and find expression in and through our lives as we touch people? In other words, how much do we have of the self-giving *agape*-type of love?

Jesus at the Door
(Rev. 3:20)

> Behold, I stand at the door and knock; if any one hears my voice and opens the door, I will come in to him and eat with him, and he with me (Rev. 3:20).

There are several marvelous truths in this verse.

One is the fact that Jesus stands at the door and knocks. He knocks not only at the door of the heart of the non-Christian but also of the Christian.

Second, if He is to come in, we must open the door. He will not knock it down. He will not force Himself on anyone.

Third, we can be just as sure that if we open the door He will come in. This is true of the one who does not know Him. It is just as true for those of us who do know Him. There may be areas of our lives where He wants in or wants in more completely. If we open the door, He will come in.

Also, thank the Lord, when He comes in, He will always bring a blessing; He will eat with us, and we with Him. What a picture of the blessings of fellowship with Him!

We should remember, however, that we must open the door. There was a picture in one of my early "readers" in public school that was entitled "Jesus at the Door." You have possibly seen the picture. The striking thing about it was the fact that Jesus stood at the door and knocked; there was no latch on the outside of the door.

No, the door must be opened from within. Do we hear Him knocking? Are we willing to open the door and invite Him in?

Conclusion

There are some verses in the closing chapters of the Revelation, the last book of the Bible, which provide a suitable conclusion to these Bible treasures. One of the most unforgettable sermons I ever heard was on "the sea was no more" (Rev. 21:1). The point was that seas separate. In the New Jerusalem there will be no separation.

Furthermore, John said, "God himself . . . will wipe away every tear" from the eyes of those in the New Jerusalem. "Death shall be no more, neither shall there be mourning or crying nor pain any more, for the former things have passed away" (21:3-4).

How glorious that will be, particularly for those who have suffered a great deal in this life and have shed many tears.

Surely all of us feel like joining with John in next to the last verse of the Bible as he says, "Amen, Come, Lord Jesus!" (Rev. 22:20). Are we ready for Him to come?